DATE DUE

The Effects of Data-Processing Service Bureaus on the Practice of Public Accounting

RECENT PUBLICATIONS

BUREAU OF BUSINESS AND ECONOMIC RESEARCH

BANKING STRUCTURE IN MICHIGAN: 1945-1963
Robert F. Lanzillotti

RETAIL DECENTRALIZATION
Eli P. Cox and Leo G. Erickson

BANK ADMINISTERED POOLED EQUITY FUNDS FOR
EMPLOYEE BENEFIT PLANS
Frank L. Voorheis

THE PERFORMANCE POST AUDIT IN STATE GOVERNMENT
Lennis M. Knighton

PASSENGER TRANSPORTATION
Stanley C. Hollander

THE EFFECTS OF DATA-PROCESSING SERVICE BUREAUS ON
THE PRACTICE OF PUBLIC ACCOUNTING
Constantine Konstans

A more complete list of publications appears at the end of this volume.

The Effects of Data-Processing Service Bureaus on the Practice of Public Accounting

by

Constantine Konstans
Associate Professor of Accounting
College of Business Administration
University of Cincinnati

1968
MSU Business Studies
Bureau of Business and Economic Research
Division of Research
Graduate School of Business Administration
Michigan State University
East Lansing, Michigan

Acknowledgments

The author wishes to express his sincere thanks to Professor Gardner Jones for his valuable assistance and encouragement in the preparation of this study. In addition, a great measure of thanks is due Professors Charles Lawrence and Mary Virginia Moore for their excellent suggestions and guidance.

A special expression of thanks must go to Professor James Don Edwards, Chairman of the Department of Accounting and Financial Administration, for his moral and pecuniary support during the preparation of this study. Likewise, I am indebted to the Haskins & Sells Foundation and to the Michigan Association of Certified Public Accountants for financial assistance during the same period.

A debt of gratitude is owed to a great number of individuals and organizations for supplying ideas and data for this study. In particular, Mr. John Healy of the Service Bureau Corporation, Mr. W. H. Evans of the Association of Data Processing Service Organizations, Mr. Vance Genzlinger of Plante and Moran, Mr. Norbert Madison of Rutten, Welling and Company, Mr. William Ludwig, formerly of the Michigan Association of Certified Public Accountants, Mr. Erwin Wittus of Parker and Wittus, and Mr. Edgar I. Gerhard of Arthur Sieferman and Associates must be singled out for their contributions. In addition, Mr. and Mrs. Stuart Thomas ably assisted me through their computer programming and statistical skills.

It is only proper that I acknowledge the assistance provided by Professor Leo G. Erickson and the personnel of the Bureau of Business and Economic Research of Michigan State University in preparing this study for publication. Above all, I am deeply indebted to Professor Anne C. Garrison, Editor of the Bureau, for her meticulous and meaningful editing efforts. Professor Garrison's patience and cooperation, in this and in similar endeavors, make formidable tasks pleasant learning processes.

Finally, I wish to acknowledge the special debt I owe my wife, Sondra, for shouldering more than her share of the effort needed to complete this study.

Table of Contents

List of Tables

List of Figures

List of Appendices

I

Introduction

The purpose of this study is to determine the effects, if any, of data-processing service bureaus on the practice of public accounting. It is assumed that data-processing service bureaus are a potential aid to certified public accountants who perform various services for clients unable to justify economically their own automated data-processing installations. Foremost among these services is that of providing management with information critical to the operation of an organization. Data-processing service bureaus help to generate such information by furnishing sophisticated equipment and highly skilled personnel without requiring corresponding capital commitments or organizational alterations. These are provided in any desired mix, depending upon the problem, for the duration of a particular requirement.

If the certified public accountant employs data-processing service bureaus to service clients, one would expect to see the various services he performs, especially his advisory services, expand. In addition, changes in client mix, quality and composition of staff, gross billings, etc., may occur. Similarly, if certain elements of the data-processing service bureau industry expand their services into activities historically provided by certified public accountants, it is reasonable to expect that there may be a diminution of CPA participation in these activities, with accompanying changes in accounting practice.

To determine the validity of these expectations, I examine the assumption that data-processing service bureaus are potentially

1

effective aids for CPA's providing a wide range of services to clients, especially advisory services.

In this context, certain challenges confronting the accounting profession are evaluated in Chapter I. These challenges arise from technological advances in disciplines closely related to accounting such as mathematics, statistics, operations research, and computer technology. Until recently, the profession has largely ignored the degree of interdependence between accounting and these disciplines.

In Chapter II, I consider management's needs for information, an area of mutual interest to service bureaus and to CPAs. In addition, the CPA's advisory services and their relationship to the management information system are examined.

A description of the service bureau industry is the subject of Chapter III. This is accomplished through an examination of several general considerations, an analysis of the industry's firms, and an evaluation of the organization and operation of a typical service bureau.

Based primarily upon a review of the literature and personal interviews, the relationships between a CPA, his clients, and service bureaus are examined in Chapter IV. In contrast, the effects of these relationships upon public practice in Michigan are evaluated in Chapter V through an analysis of the responses to several question-naire surveys. The groups surveyed were the member firms of the Michigan Association of Certified Public Accountants, service bureaus operating in Michigan, and a sample of Michigan commercial banks.

In Chapter VI, two topics which may have profound effects on the future of the public accounting profession receive a cursory examination. The first is the entrance of commercial banks into the service bureau industry. The second is the multiple-access-computer service bureau, a revolutionary new concept in service bureau employment.

SCOPE OF THE STUDY

The major portion of the study's empirical research is limited geographically to Michigan. However, its applicability need not be restricted geographically because the literature reviewed is not limited to Michigan nor is a portion of the empirical research consisting of interviews and correspondence. In addition, the study relates to the role of the CPA as a provider and interpreter of information. As such, it emphasizes the CPA's advisory function because of its relationship to the management information system.

BACKGROUND

When the history of our age is written, I think it will record three profoundly important technological developments;

Nuclear energy, which tremendously increases the amount of *energy* available to do the world's work;

Automation, which greatly increases man's ability to use *tools;*

And computers, which multiply man's ability to do *mental work.* Some of our engineers believe that of the three, the computer will bring the greatest benefit to man.[1]

The words of Ralph J. Cordiner, formerly chairman of the board of directors of the General Electric Company, have implications the public accounting profession cannot ignore. Multiplying man's ability to perform mental work implies creative and imaginative thinking, a pursuit fundamental to the survival of any profession in our rapidly changing economic environment. Certainly, creative and imaginative thinking, resting on a foundation of integrity, is the essence of the public accounting profession's service to the economy.

The computer's impact on the accounting profession has been the subject of great concern to the American Institute of Certified Public Accountants (AICPA).

For more than a year the Institute has been studying various aspects of a big problem—how computers will affect accounting practice. The more it is studied, the bigger the problem grows. The only answer so far is that the impact will be tremendous—soon.[2]

This was the dominant theme during the Institute's annual meeting in 1965. In recent issues of the Institute's publications, the impact of the computer on the profession has been highly publicized. The following are examples:

If we don't master the computer, it could destroy us. If we do master the computer, it will give us an abundantly creative instrument with which to work.[3]

If they (CPAs) make an ally of the computer, it will assist them to achieve an even higher level of eminence; and if they ignore or resist it, they will pay a terrible price in lost prestige.[4]

These warnings are ominous, but timely. There is great fear, however, that these warnings are not being heeded. In this context,

Trueblood suggests that "complacency could be our undoing, if we permit it to take hold."[5]

THE CHALLENGE

These warnings are in a sense misleading and lacking in perspective. The computer, per se, is not the fundamental challenge facing the profession. The fundamental challenge is that the computer permits the effective integration of related disciplines and the more intensive utilization of the knowledge of a single discipline for solving an assortment of problems. A new science has thus been created,

. . . concerned with the problems of classifying, processing and interpreting information. This science encompasses a field including such subjects as widely divergent as bookkeeping and cybernetics, neurology and operational research, standard costing and servomechanisms. This new science has been rather tentatively christened Information Technology.[6]

As the knowledge boundaries of information technology expand, professional engagements relying exclusively upon traditional accounting methodology may result in tomorrow's CPA and information technologist having the same relationship as today's bookkeeper and CPA.

Information technology, through the electronic computer, presents the public accounting profession with a three-part challenge related to reporting financial history, preparing and analyzing decision-making information, and auditing.

Reporting Financial History

The CPA's role as a reporter of financial history consists of determining the necessary financial information needed by the many diverse but interested parties, designing an effective system (including the underlying procedures and methods needed to provide this information efficiently) and presenting this information within stated time-limits, in a usable or prescribed form, consistent with generally accepted accounting principles.

The first phase of the fiduciary function, determining the financial information requirements of the diverse interest groups, is simultaneously aided and made more complicated. The computer allows the rapid and relatively inexpensive processing of vast quantities of data into many useful forms. Consequently, the economic reasons for allowing the information requirements of various parties to remain unsatisfied are no longer valid. However, before machines can produce anything of value, they must be supplied with something potentially valuable. Such a requirement forces the accountant to ascertain which items of financial information are relevant to each group's needs. This is a relatively uncomplicated exercise in the assumption-rich world of theory, but it demands great expertise in practice.

Because the information needs of the various interested parties are different, accounting methodology attempts to adapt. The second phase, that pertaining to the design of the system for collecting and processing financial data and presenting information, has been changed time after time to reflect such factors as Securities and Exchange Commission requirements, tax law modifications, and internal requirements such as the implementation of standard costing. The trend has been in the direction of more financial information and of more relevant and timely financial information, especially for internal uses. Reflecting this trend, accountants with foresight designed new systems which, in each succeeding modification phase, often substituted automated equipment for manual methods. Generally, systems became progressively more efficient and complex.

The third phase, that of information presentation, has been greatly improved, certainly in terms of punctuality. In addition, the computer's capabilities allow the preparation of reports more analytical in nature. For example, income statements with year-to-date and current account balances and percentages are easily prepared, as are a variety of exception-type reports.

Preparing and Analyzing Quantitative Information for Decision Making

All relevant information necessary for decision making is not necessarily financial in nature. The computer facilitates, economically and physically, the accumulation of quantitative data such as machine running times, number of sub-assemblies completed, or units of raw material in process of conversion. Often such seemingly obscure variables or other variables expressed in terms or functions of tons, yards, passenger-miles, etc., are the key to profitability for a firm. The CPA must realize the importance of this type of data and incorporate its capture, preparation, and presentation into the information system in order that he may remain management's information specialist. The typical financially oriented information system does not always accumulate such data. When it does, these data are often obscure by-products of the primary financial data flow.

An even graver challenge confronts the CPA. Information technology challenges the accountant's role as an analyst of information for decision making because the computer permits the application of operations research techniques to rapid and relatively precise analysis of various problems. These techniques make it possible to take into consideration more variables than when utilizing the traditional accounting techniques, to assign values to variables heretofore unquantifiable and hence ignored, to assign probabilities to the future values of variables, and to develop alternatives and thus make possible the selection of an optimal solution. In contrast, the accountant has traditionally relied on relatively imprecise arithmetical relationships that often produce ambiguous results.

Auditing a Computerized System

The third challenge to the accountant relates to his role as auditor. Information technology can be of use to management generally through the availability of a computer, inhouse or outside, to collect and process data, and to present information. As a client's needs and recognition of these needs become more acute, there is pressure to acquire sophisticated equipment commensurate with these needs. The auditor soon finds his traditional "audit trail" obliterated as "real-time" computers are adopted. Not having available, all at one time, the various source documents, journals, ledgers, summaries, and financial statements presents problems unlike those ever before encountered.

At the apparent heart of these problems is the fact that the computer, "with its never ending flow of improvements, represents something foreboding and mysterious to those concerned with controls over information processing."[7] However, more fundamental may be the fact that the auditor imperfectly understands the concept of control. Many engineers, systems analysts, and programmers believe this, and hence consider the auditor unqualified to judge a computerized information system's reliability. If their contentions are true, the auditor's task should be sharply curtailed. Perhaps some other source, upon whom the auditor would rely, should determine the information system's degree of reliability.

The auditor would then merely fulfill the requirements as expressed in the Securities Exchange Act of 1934. However, if the internal control phase of the attest function is abdicated and if it is agreed that exclusive reliance on financial information is inadequate for satisfying the CPA's advisory function, then today's CPA has no basis for his claim to the role of management's information specialist. It may be that the information he presents is often neither reliable nor relevant.

To meet this challenge, the CPA must develop his capabilities as an information technologist by becoming proficient in disciplines related to accounting, such as economics and mathematics. But to do this effectively he should avoid a common pitfall: specialization within a discipline to the complete exclusion of the other component areas. A measure of true proficiency in a given discipline is the ability to interrelate that discipline with others. However, this can often be best accomplished when the ability to interrelate the components of one discipline is developed and demonstrated.

II

Management Services and the
Information Needs of Clients

Individuals trained in the discipline of accounting have at some point in their education encountered the phrases "accounting is the language of business" and "accounting is information." Unqualified, these phrases are ambiguous: it might be assumed that all business information is expressed in monetary terms, or all business information is historical in nature. There could be further assumptions about the effectiveness of accounting in communicating management's decisions to the appropriate organizational elements, or as to the lack of any limitations upon accounting's ability to control a giant corporation. In fact, any number of assumptions, many of them clearly erroneous, attach to these phrases. Bierman implicitly recognizes this by stating, "accounting is *a* language of business. . . ."[1] (Emphasis added.) Elliott and Wasley go further and assert, "*statistical business data* constitute the 'language of business' "[2] (Emphasis added.)

Bierman's qualification questions the implication that accounting data are the sole form of business information. He considers accounting data important, but he implicitly recognizes the existence of other unspecified sources.[3] Elliott and Wasley dispel the notion that accounting enjoys a special distinction as a form of business information by recognizing that reports based on a wide variety of data, financial and non-financial, are deemed useful by management.[4]

In order to examine the implications raised, the CPA's management services function is here related to a client's information

8

needs. To do this, I review the nature of information and of management information. Then I explore the objective of accounting, and relate the status of managerial accounting to management's information needs. Finally, the concept of a management information system is developed and related to the CPA's advisory role, i.e. the management services function.

THE NATURE OF INFORMATION

Information is the basic ingredient of decision making. As the situations in which decisions must be made become more complex, the need for information correspondingly increases. And it has been characteristic of modern life that it is complex. Business, science and technology, government—each is concerned with a world encompassing more and more interrelationships, and the need in each case has therefore become even greater to provide the decision maker with more information.[5]

The need for information has not gone unrecognized. It has been estimated that 60,000 books, 100,000 research treatises, and 1,300,000 articles are published throughout the world.[6] Nor is this "information explosion" limited exclusively to sources outside the boundaries of organizations. The torrent of internally-generated information has reached massive proportions as various items of automated equipment replace manual clerical methods. Of course, the information explosion is not without concomitant problems for the potential beneficiaries. Information storage, retrieval, and dissemination problems become highly complex. In addition, even the definition of relevant information, that information necessary for effective decision making, is obscured by the sheer quantity of information actually and potentially available.

Before favorable effects from increased information can accrue to the decision-maker, he should understand the nature of information. This may be accomplished by distinguishing between information and data, reviewing the qualities of information, and analyzing the essence of managerial information.

Information and Data

Information is a subset of data in that all information is data, but not all data are information.[7] Gregory and Van Horn state that "the word data may be used to cover all types of facts obtained; the term information is useful for denoting the particular facts management wants to know."[8] A meaningful amplification of the preceding statement may be that information pertains to the facts management *needs to know* in order to perform its two most important functions, planning and controlling.

The differences between data and information are subtle, but nonetheless important. Data represent all facts gathered about events or circumstances, while information evolves only after selected data, when combined or otherwise processed into some unique form, exhibit certain qualities. To provide information, emphasis must be placed upon the attainment of these qualities rather than upon indiscriminate data collection and processing. An examination of these qualities may assist in better understanding the composition of managerial information.

Quality of Information

The quality of information has several dimensions. Among these are accuracy, timeliness, predictability, relevance, completeness, quantifiability and availability.

Accuracy. Accuracy is a measure of reliability or perfection, the ". . . long-run ratio of correct answers to total answers that comprise information. . . ."[9] Information serves as the basis for operating decisions and hence its degree of reliability affects the results of decisions. Undesirable results come about when inaccuracies in information are caused by factors such as human error, equipment malfunction, or a poorly conceived network of related procedures which fail to combine stored information and data pertaining to current operating events.

However, accuracy has a cost. Error control can be implemented by human inspectors, check digits in account numbers, parallel circuitry in computers or checks designed into a computer program. Each method has a theoretical value: the favorable results attained. However, at some point the value attributable to control devices will be less than their cost, and all succeeding equal increments of control cost may account for continuously diminishing increments of value. For some applications, management will decide to stop short of this point, but for others it can accept only an infinitesimal degree of error.

Timeliness. Timeliness enhances the quality of information in the sense of its being available at some desired point in time. "Timeliness, or the age of information, has three components: interval, delay, and reporting time."[10] Interval is the time period between the start of successive preparations of information in report form. It can be a constant as in weekly reports, or it can be variable as in special purpose reports. Delay time refers to the time period from the point additional transactions are not accepted for inclusion in a particular report to the dissemination of the report to users. This time-period is composed of the cumulative time necessary for data processing, report preparation, and delivery. The reporting period is the time-period covered by the report and, for regularly recurring reports, it is usually equal to and coincident with the interval. These relationships are illustrated schematically in Figure II-1.

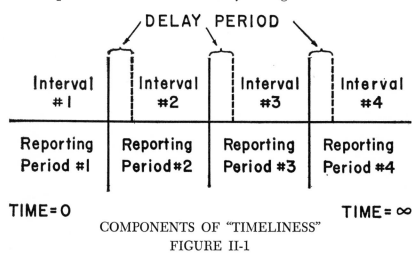

COMPONENTS OF "TIMELINESS"
FIGURE II-1

Predictability. Information pertains to a continuum of events which, in terms of management's knowledge of these, is bounded by two absolutes, certainty and uncertainty. Clearly, detailed information is more readily available for relatively certain or predictable events than for those whose possible outcomes are more obscure. However, detailed information is often more valuable with respect to uncertain events. It is here that decision making takes on crucial dimensions because there is the greatest probability of making a sub-optimal decision without having all the facts. For relatively predictable events, detailed information quickly attains a negative value.

Relevance. For facts to be classified as information, they must be pertinent to the problem confronting the receiver; and only when considered in relation to the receiver's previously accumulated information, prior experience, and degree of analytical sophistication, do facts acquire an informational content.

Concern for informational relevance comes after three levels of communication are satisfied. The first deals with the accuracy of the information conveyed in terms of the identity or equivalence of the received symbols and the symbols used by the sender in describing an event. The second is the precision by which the received symbols cover the intended meaning. The final level relates to the observable recipient reaction to the symbols received. For information to be relevant, it must bear upon or be usefully associated with the action it is designed to facilitate or the result it is desired to produce.[11]

The user's point of view must also be considered. "The main point here is precisely that information is management information only to the extent to which the manager needs or wants it; and it is significant to him only in terms of its relation. . . to his personal responsibility."[12] Similarly, facts obtained about events the receiver cannot control through his actions are often irrelevant data rather than information.

Completeness. Incomplete information about an event is often, for decision-making purposes, more serious than a complete lack of information. Perfect knowledge or information is one of the important simplifying assumptions of micro-economic theory; but it is understandably not appropriate other than for analytical purposes. Consequently, management must at all times recognize that even the most seemingly complete information lacks completeness because of the costs associated with improving the sophistication of an existing information system and the limits placed by existing technology on possible improvements. Efforts to produce information which is more complete should be directed to those areas where the pay-off is greatest. The quality of completeness also introduces the concept of judgment and illustrates that this human factor must be always present to evaluate all information received, in order to verify that it is indeed information, before basing a decision on it.

Quantifiability. The quantification or measurement of data adds to its usefulness. The more sophisticated the method of measurement, the more useful are the data in terms of informational content.

Measurement in its most primitive aspect involves forming classes of equivalent objects or events. This is the basis of identifying, recognizing, and labeling ordinary objects. Moving up the scale of measurement, more information is communicated about the items measured. Progression is from statements of equality (within classes) through knowledge of greater than or less than (or positional relationships) to statements about the magnitude of differences, and finally to ratios. Thus quantification conveys more information than strictly qualitative statements. . . .[13]

Information which is developed through increasingly sophisticated methods of quantification may enhance the receiver's ability for decision making, which in turn reflects upon the operations for which he bears responsibility.

Availability. Only available information has a positive influence on decision making. Consequently, in an effective reporting system, making available the information deemed necessary for decision making is a very important consideration. Most items of internal information can be generated if management is willing to pay the price. Remote data collection devices, vast information storage units with rapid retrieval capabilities, and "real-time" computers are accomplishing phenomenal results in this respect. On the other hand, desired external data are frequently difficult to acquire. For example, the pricing policies of competitors are usually closely guarded. Such data, together with internal data on a newly proposed product, would result in information useful to a new-product-introduction decision. The problem then becomes that of finding useful substitute information already available or derivable by such tools as market research studies. By constant development of new tools, data previously unobtainable are acquired. But, as of a given point in time, potential information is not information until it is available for aiding decision making.

Managerial Information

For every enterprise there is a unique set of discernible variables which are of utmost importance to management if it is to perform effectively its primary functions of planning and control. Consequently, information relating to these variables and exhibiting the qualities discussed is an essential item upon which to base decisions. While the set of variables may often appear identical in firms in similar lines, this identity is superficial. One variable which will affect the perception of and the reaction to all other variables is always different between firms. That variable is people.

It is useful to differentiate these variables as internal and external and financial and nonfinancial. Singly each variable is important, but it is often more meaningful to consider them in terms of their relative importance to operations and in terms of the degree of control which can be exercised over them.

Internal financial variables are those which determine return on investment or earning power. These are sales volume, selling price, product mix, all costs, and investment in all classes of assets. Internal non-financial variables may include the quality of personnel and recruiting policy; the firm's reporting system and its responsiveness; and the age of equipment, its efficient utilization, and the labor/capital employment ratio. External financial variables would include the conditions of the money and capital markets and official policy affecting these. Non-financial external variables are such factors as consumer tastes and preferences, conditions in the factor markets, and technological advances.

As between financial and non-financial variables, the latter may be more difficult to recognize and consequently there may be less available information pertaining to them. (The dearth of information relative to these variables may reflect upon the accountant in that the established information system is essentially financial in nature). Because non-financial variables are often more critical than the financial variables with which they interact, management must be informed about them. Neuschel notes:

For any business—large or small—these [non-financial variables] will ordinarily consist of not more than four to six factors. They are the activities or aspects of the business that have a major impact, not only on short-term profit results, but also on long-term growth and competitive strength. As such they are the more important because they represent the only means through which the key financial variables . . . can be influenced or changed.[14]

These factors vary more widely from industry to industry than do the financial variables. For example, in the automobile industry, car-styling and the effectiveness of the dealer force are important; for the chemical industry, the important factors include new product research and the development of new uses for existing products.[15]

Accounting, considered as the language of business and synonymous with information, must supply management with information on variables critical to overall operations regardless of their source or nature. If it does not, the accountant will not remain management's chief information specialist.

THE EFFECTIVENESS OF ACCOUNTING
AS A PROVIDER OF INFORMATION

The accounting profession has been greatly affected by our nation's rapid economic growth. One result is the profession's increased prominence in economic affairs. Another is with the difficulty inherent in absorbing new developments while digesting older ones. Underlying the second result is the ever present problem of ascertaining the true objective of accounting. No matter how obscure this problem may be made to appear when thrust into the background by considerations judged temporarily more critical, it is fundamental to the profession's existence.

The Objective of Accounting

It is submitted that *the fundamental objective of accounting is to provide a continuous source of information exhibiting the qualities of accuracy, timeliness, predictability, relevance, completeness, quantifiability and availability relating to critical internal and external variables, financial and non-financial in nature. Further, the time dimensions of this information should include past, present, and (for internal reporting purposes only) anticipated events in the life of a business enterprise, useful to the various parties maintaining an economic interest therein, upon which they may base future actions.*

This statement of objective is not in complete accord with earlier definitions of accounting, as for instance:

Accounting is the art of recording, classifying and summarizing in a significant manner and in terms of money, transactions and events which are, in part at least, of a financial character, and interpreting the results thereof.[16]

This definition emphasizes the accountant's stewardship role and implies adherence to standardized reporting practices and conventions which often work against the accountant as he provides information for managerial decision making. Trueblood cites the advent of LIFO as one example of this dilemma.[17] Another cited is in the design of cost systems.

It is questionable whether a useful cost accounting system can or needs be tied into the accountant's over-all principle of historical costs. Perhaps an improved concept of cost accounting would be one involving theories of replacement and opportunity cost. . .[18]

The objectives of accounting implied by many older definitions of the discipline thus create a basic misconception of the complexities involved in managing a business enterprise and of the potential role of accounting as an aid to decision making. What management needs is information pertinent to the job at hand, not standardized reporting procedures supported by often conflicting alternative conventions invoked for the purpose of complying with the concept of stewardship.

These comments are not meant to urge de-emphasis of traditional functions. Instead, their positive informational content should be emphasized. Financial accounting should provide information on the present position and past operations of the enterprise tailored to the needs of interested parties. Information of this type may require such concepts as general and specific price-level adjustments, and distinctions between operating profit and holding gains to be incorporated in financial reports.[19] Taxing authorities should receive information peculiar to their requirements without affecting the discharge of the other functions except as they provide useful information for investment decisions, capital expenditures, etc. In addition, the attest function should provide assurances to the various parties that the information received is reliable and adequately descriptive of economic reality. The auditor's statement as to reliability guards against the degeneration of the existing information system and his assurance that the information is adequately descriptive of economic reality protects the reporting system from obsolescence.[20]

Managerial Accounting and Management's Information Needs

In the early 20th century, the scientific management revolution found the discipline of accounting an effective means for communicating information to management relative to operational events.[21] However, one important modification had to be made. Accounting had to shift its emphasis from the past to the present and future in order that management could use the communicated information for planning and control. Accountants developed useful techniques such as standard costing, direct costing, flexible budgets, responsibility accounting, and cost-volume-profit analyses. Originally non-financial information was accepted and recast into financial terms. Current events were compared to anticipated projections. All levels of management decision making were aided by developments such as cost-variance reports and product-line profitability analyses.

Today, the complexities inherent in large-scale operations have created a dissatisfaction with the available managerial information. The accounting techniques in use are considered inadequate for generating the desired managerial information.

It is ironic that managerial accounting is criticized at a time when it has apparently broken loose from many of the constraining external reporting conventions which bind financial accounting. However, when one examines managerial accounting critically, strong adherence to the monetary convention is found to persist. Accounting information is still synonymous with financial information. If managerial accounting is to be considered essentially an information system and if the accountant is to be considered as management's information specialist, "it is increasingly difficult for the accountant to accept responsibility for one set of financial data without becoming involved with a larger and larger share of the organization's information function."[22] Given such developments as electronic computers and analytical tools such as operations research, the line between accounting and non-accounting information becomes increasingly tenuous. In reality there is a single pool of data from which to derive managerial information. To stop short of providing management with all the decision-making information needed may imply that the managerial accounting function will some day only provide data for inclusion within an information report prepared by some unspecified party, presumably not an accountant. Such an outcome distressingly resembles the task of the present-day plant bookkeeper laboriously preparing detailed data for inclusion in the plant accountant's variance report.

MANAGEMENT INFORMATION SYSTEMS

It is becoming apparent that managerial accounting must move beyond the traditional boundaries which restrict its usefulness. A broader concept of managerial accounting is needed which will embrace all activities involved in gathering managerial information. Such a concept opens the way for the accountant's transition to becoming a true information technologist, thus maintaining his position as management's information specialist. To accomplish this, there is need for a vehicle to coordinate the various activities and skills inherent in such a role. The management or business information system is that vehicle. Before examining the concept of a management or business information system, it may be useful to trace the development of the systems concept and the related technological advancements in business-oriented computers.

The Systems Concept in Business

The systems concept in business has been in transition since its early days, some twenty-five years ago.[23] Its beginnings reflect its heritage from the Taylorian scientific management movement, which in turn draws from thoughts centuries old. Then as now, many industrial engineers were engaged in the field. Such factors as forms, files, office equipment, and personnel were coordinated through standardized procedures in order to combine, simplify, and improve repetitive clerical operations involving several people within an organizational department. Techniques such as time and motion studies, flow charts, organization charts, and office layout diagrams were also used. However, the emphasis was placed almost solely on paperwork improvements and only portions of a problem were considered rather than the problem in its entirety. "To illustrate, a study might be made of a credit handling problem without recognizing its relationship or impact on an order system of which it was a vital part."[24] Systems concepts were obviously influenced greatly by the functional organization structure.

The next step occurred with the development of procedures for unifying a particular process without concern for intra-organizational boundaries. Procedures involving more than one department were devised for such sub-systems as sales and cash receipts, purchasing and cash disbursements, timekeeping and payroll, and inventory and production control. DeLuca refers to this as the "total procedures stage," to differentiate it from the previous stage in which intra-organizational boundaries were considered almost sacrosanct.[25] The total procedures stage became practical when technological developments allowed the multiple use of input data. The phrase, "capture once," became a byword in systems work. However, "this concept was concentrated on operational improvements, rather than on management information requirements."[26] Furthermore, as the rigidity inherent in business information systems due to the influence of the organization structure began to disappear, there appeared a new rigidity influenced by the equipment introduced as a part of the system. Each application had to be explicitly defined and only specially trained personnel could perform certain jobs.

A more subtle approach to business systems, the "total systems" concept, has developed. The fundamental difference between this and the total procedures stage is conceptual. The total systems approach views the organization as a bundle of resources in terms of capital, labor, etc., and is interested in their interactions while continuing the de-emphasis of the functional organizational framework of finance, production and sales.

By moving beyond the total procedures stage, or as Genzlinger terms it, the "integrated systems stage," one leaves a stage imbued predominately with a middle-management-oriented frame of reference, concerned with the control of processes which cross organizational boundaries but where information interrelating these processes is a relatively minor consideration.[27] Entering the total systems phase, a top management viewpoint is mandatory. The emphasis shifts to providing the information required to formulate organizational plans and to facilitate organizational control through integrating the various sub-systems.

However, the total systems concept has a major disadvantage. Orientation to the output requirements of the various sub-systems, which implies separate handling of common data, raises problems of equipment efficiency, information timeliness, and inter-sub-system reconciliation.[28] Because each sub-system has its own data-generating capabilities, each must have its own data storage facilities. For common items of data, this represents redundant storage. Furthermore, the requirement for data transmission between sub-systems affects data timeliness and represents inefficient use of equipment. When equipment is busy transferring data, it cannot concurrently update stored data based on new events. In addition, due to possible variations in the degree of data timeliness between sub-systems, reports reaching management reflecting the integration of data from several sub-systems may be internally inconsistent in terms of time. Instead of a clear picture of the situation, management will have a picture blurred by data from different time dimensions.

Recently a new business system concept, the "single information flow" approach, has been proposed.

The single information flow concept might be likened to the efficient one-man storekeeper, who came quite close to ultimate real-time random-access information handling. The cans on the shelf and a few pencil marks gave him both inventory and purchasing information; the book next to the cash drawer provided accounts receivable, credit and customer information; the bank book plus cash drawer gave him his cash balance; and accounts payable were visible on the nail on which he spindled the bills.[29]

The basic philosophy underlying this approach is that all necessary information must be available in only one place in the system and for all uses. As opposed to the output-oriented total systems concept, the single information flow concept is input-oriented. It concentrates on collecting the essential data into a common storage facility and from there servicing the information needs of everyone in the firm. Other characteristics of this concept are that it satisfies the basic data requirements, to include both transactions and results of decisions, for the appropriate managerial level and position in the firm; and it provides secondary or "off-line" processing and storage facilities for information relevant only to a segment of the firm.[30] Obviously, very sophisticated programs, computers, and items of peripheral equipment are needed to implement this concept.

The Role of the Computer

The more advanced information system concepts discussed are possible without the computer, but usually they are not very practicable. Much depends upon the scale and complexity of a firm's operations. However, the developments in computer technology have stimulated the growth and importance of the systems concept in business. In fact, the various improvements in commercial, as opposed to scientific, computers can be loosely associated with the various levels in the development of that concept.

Developments prior to 1954. Prior to the introduction of the first electronic computer into business, the most advanced items of equipment available for automating data processing activities were tabulating or unit record machines. These machines are still very much used by various types of organizations.

Tabulating machines are used very effectively in conjunction with equipment which produces punched-paper tape as a by-product. For example, in operations such as order and billing, a paper tape produced at the initial order writing "captures" inventory, receivables, sales, cost of sales, and sales analysis data. The tape is then converted into punched cards for processing by the tabulating equipment.

The capabilities of this equipment strongly influenced the development of the "total procedures" or "integrated systems" stage. Information systems, actually a group of sub-systems such as the sales and cash receipts sub-system, were designed, using tabulating equipment to handle the routine, repetitive data processing tasks. The equipment's economic justification was the reduction of clerical personnel and a concurrent reduction in paperwork. Although these benefits often did not materialize, systems designers were given comparatively sophisticated equipment to incorporate into their designs. It appears that advances in equipment were instrumental in allowing the systems concept to reduce the influence of the functional organization structure. Systems designers were given the means to expand the concepts inherent in manual equipment, such as the three-position writing board which streamlined operations within a department, to larger segments of the firm. In effect, tabulating equipment became to the various sub-systems what the writing board was to the check-writing operation.

The electronic computer. The outstanding characteristic of the electronic computer which distinguishes it from tabulating equipment is an internally stored program, a set of operating instructions inserted into the machine in the same way and place as data to be processed. The computer's control is the program. The program is analogous to the control board found in tabulating equipment: it controls data input, storage, manipulation and output. However, the computer's program, acting through electrical circuitry conceptually based on the logic of Boolean algebra, allows the computer a limited degree of self-direction. The self-directing capability permits a great degree of sophistication in computer applications. Many applications fail to utilize this potential. The computer was and still is often considered a super tabulating machine, useful for expediting the performance of clerical operations.

The electronic computer, due in part at least to its processing and data retrieval speeds, was an important factor in refining the integrated systems concept and in the evolution to the direction of the total systems stage.

Many fine examples of integrated systems were developed. Card and paper tape punches were added to nearly all document writing devices to provide automatic inputs. Magnetic tape units were added to the computer. The turnaround document was perfected. Computer outputs were designed to become input after adjustments and additions were made.[31]

But unfortunately the computer was usually superimposed upon the existing system, merely taking over the functions of manual methods or tabulating equipment.

The system designers seem to have adopted the point of view that it is possible to put a Cadillac engine in a Model-T; that the computer is compatible with existing systems except insofar as the links between machine-sensible input and output are concerned.[32]

This situation has been furthered by at least two other considerations. First, it is easier to justify a computer to management economically, in terms of cost savings, than by assigning values expressed in dollar amounts to the intangible benefits inherent in improved information. Everyone understands the economic significance of a reduction in force, but the benefits from better decisions are more difficult to perceive. Emphasis on cost savings leads to considering the proposed computer simply as a replacement for existing manual methods or tabulating equipment. Secondly, the state of computer technology was characterized until recently by capabilities limited to processing data in accumulated groups (batch-processing) where a particular job had to be completely processed before another could begin. The great majority of computers in business use today have this characteristic. Consequently, information pertinent to concurrent operations, as between two dependent sub-systems, is often not available quickly enough to be useful for controlling operations. Therefore it is submitted that these two considerations help to explain the absence of true systems modifications and the concomitant suboptimal equipment use when firms acquire a computer. Futhermore, the continued employment of the integrated procedures concept or the transition to the total systems concept, but no further, is a logical outcome, given these considerations.

Recent developments. Recent technological advances in computers, peripheral equipment, communications devices, and programming techniques have aided in the development of computerized informations systems which have concretized the abstraction, *high quality information.* Clerical cost reduction is a consideration secondary to newer equipment configurations which feature "random access devices, remote inquiry and data generation stations, automatic interrupt of processing and immediate response."[33] These computers are controlled by an executive routine, a special computer program which allows them to perform simultaneously the operations of data input, search of storage, data manipulation, and output. Control considerations have priority over processing; therefore, control information, such as feedback results of a decision, interrupts the processing of payroll or of an operations research application. Stored information or "files" are updated instantaneously as events occur rather than at some future point as in batch-processing.

In such a system the computer is in a position to acquire information covering thousands of occurrences such as orders of products, receipts of raw materials, break-downs of equipment, production of parts, engineering changes, and so forth. This information can be analyzed and compared with plans; and situations that require attention can be brought to the attention of the proper person in time for him to take corrective action.[34]

In addition, aided by operations research techniques, the computer will often choose the most effective alternative and implement that alternative automatically. Items of equipment possessing these capabilities are a prerequisite for implementing the single information flow concept. The advent of such equipment and the emergence of the single information flow concept further underscores the important interaction between technological advances in equipment and the development of information systems concepts.

The Concept of a Management Information System

Management information systems are ill-defined conceptually, as evidenced by the "lack of either a general theory for design or, in lieu of such a theory, a broad base of qualified experience."[35] Writers seem to confuse systems concepts, equipment configurations, and operational functions with the concept of a management information system. This confusion has resulted in "a plethora of descriptive techniques and a number of pedestrian descriptions of a business (management) information system."[36]

Every firm has a management information system with its ultimate goal being "to keep all levels of management completely informed on all developments in the business which affect them."[37] Regardless of the scale or complexity of operations, from the word-of-mouth information characteristic of a small proprietorship to giant corporations where machines communicate with one another without human intervention, it is submitted that underlying the ultimate goal of the management information system is the concept of tailoring that system to accommodate a unique set of individuals referred to as management. This concept recognizes the innate differences in the abilities of individuals to perceive, assimilate and decide. Of course, most systems fall far short of the ultimate goal.

Basically, the concept of tailoring a system involves a compromise between several factors which should dominate systems design considerations. These factors are:

1. The *absolute minimum* amount of information needed to plan and control operations to the degree necessary for the firm to remain in business, given the firm's management, other resources, competition, and the state of the arts.

2. The *maximum* amount of information the firm's management is capable of comprehending and effectively using, limited by the firm's resources and the state of information technology.

3. That amount of information *theoretically possible,* limited only by the state of information technology.

Factor One establishes the conceptual "floor" in the systems designer's quest for adequate information while Factor Three sets the "ceiling" or ideal. Factor Two represents the attainable and as such becomes the standard. Factor Two must at no time be lower than Factor One and cannot technically exceed Factor Three. Given this condition, the conceptual design rule becomes as follows: design a system maximizing management's inherent capabilities and the firm's other resources within the boundary of available technology, but never allow the quantity of information generated to fall below a level necessary to maintain the firm's ability to compete.

This concept does not specify the systems approach to adopt or the degree of desired automation. It says nothing about how to organize a firm or which personnel selection policy to consider. But it strongly implies the following:

There is a finite limit to which systems development can be carried, and every company must decide for itself at what point that limit will be reached. *You cannot simply transplant a system from one company to another* [emphasis added]. Not only are the systems requirements different from company to company but also the ability to perfect all management skills, including systematization, will not be the same in any two companies. Models from other companies, books, or computer manufacturer manuals may be helpful as checklists or guides, but the major portions of the system have to be especially designed to meet the needs of [a] business and its managers.[38]

With respect to a system's equipment requirements, let it be stressed that while sophisticated computer installations are often required, these are a function of the scale and complexity of operations. Excellent management information systems can be designed and serviced by a local data processing service bureau. In many instances manual methods would suffice. In fact, the irrational importance attributed to computers ("computeritis") is said to be one of the major obstacles to establishing a management information system.[39]

In order to provide management with information necessary for planning and controlling operations, the management information system, being the information-providing vehicle of the information technologist, draws from various disciplines.[40] Economic theory, organization theories, accounting, information theory, communication theory, mathematics, statistics, and operations research add to the conceptual framework of a management information system. In addition, the tools of operations research such as network theory, mathematical programming, and probabilistic and simulation models assist systems designers in improving overall system quality by finding and investigating the many interrelationships existing in a firm.

The decision rule developed earlier, the equipment, and the knowledge drawn from various disciplines must be based upon a framework composed of certain essential elements. These elements are:

1. *The firm's objectives.* What does management wish to accomplish with the resources under its control and the restrictions it may be subject to?

2. *Alternative approaches to accomplish objectives.* For example, a profit objective may be attained by adjustments in margin or turnover.

3. *Standards to measure the relative efficiency of the various alternatives in attaining an objective.* For example, margin and/or turnover adjustments must consider the cost aspects underlying an alternative. One approach may be more efficient than all others to accomplish an objective. Management must be informed which alternative that is.

4. *Guidelines for attaining objectives.* A firm can successfully attain a profit objective by sharp practices only in the short run, due in part to customer alienation. In addition to delineating an objective, considerations as to how to attain it should be specified.

5. *Clear division of guidelines among the functional components of the organization.* The consideration involved here is that in order to attain the firm's objectives, functional elements must be controlled. With each element assigned a specified portion of a guideline, its operations can be controlled more effectively. This is essential because the firm's optimal performance involves a balance between the efforts of its

functional components, not a summation of their efforts. Implied here is the fact that one or more elements may have to suboptimize their own performance in order to optimize the firm's performance.

6. *A mechanism for comparing actual operations with established standards.* Included therein would be the ability to feed back the effects of prior operations and the results of non-human routine decision-making on the state of the system. In addition, the mechanism should be able to signal for human intervention when automatic controls fail to adhere to established standards or because of a requirement for a non-routine decision.

7. *Adequate system controls.* The system should be so designed that the firm's assets are adequately protected and the operations subject to review.[41]

These elements, which help determine the design of the management information system, are themselves not easily determined. Adequate planning underlies their realization from the start to the finish of a management information system installation program. Burroughs Corporation developed a useful 10-point action list for determining these elements when they inaugurated a five-year program, in 1962, aimed at developing and implementing their management information system.

These are:

1. Appreciate the limitations of existing "hardware."
2. Challenge all existing procedures and ways of doing things.
3. Define the system's needs by having the individual managers formalize their own needs.
4. Elicit positive sympathetic leadership from management.
5. Educate and motivate all levels of management as to the importance of such a program.
6. Insist on a single integrated system concerned with all of the relationships within the system. Do not start with the accounting function when designing the system. Concentrate initially upon the basic data pertaining to people and products and their activities and movement. The pay-off is highest here.
7. Control the implementation centrally but allow active participation by all levels of management.
8. Employ adequate amounts of resources. The effectiveness of resources is found to be approximately equal to their square. Hence a dissipation of resources occurs when inadequate amounts are employed.
9. Integrate management and operations with the system.
10. Plan and schedule in minute detail. Tools such as PERT should be used to monitor the whole of the development and implementation phase.[42]

THE PUBLIC ACCOUNTANT'S MANAGEMENT SERVICES ROLE

Clients of public accounting firms are increasingly aware of the developments in systems concepts and technology, and of the capabilities of the accountant as an information technologist. Many clients are not large enough to provide this assistance to themselves. Larger clients find the paucity of skilled personnel a problem. Many are turning to their CPA for advice on management information systems to include systems design and equipment selection.

In the spring of 1961, the Council of the American Institute of Certified Public Accountants adopted the following resolution:

It is an objective of the Institute, recognizing that management service activities are a proper function of CPAs, to encourage all CPAs to perform the entire range of management services consistent with their professional competence, ethical standards and responsibility.[43]

As Carey notes, there is no currently available definition of the term "management services" let alone a conceptual foundation. The lack of a definition, however, had not stifled many firms' expansion of services beyond auditing and tax prior to the Council's pronouncement. In order to aid management with the burgeoning problems posed by conversion to peace-time production following World War II, many firms which previously viewed the field of management services with skepticism were forced to provide their clients with more assistance beyond audit and tax services. Even more important, "management now began to express a clear-cut dissatisfaction with the accounting firm which limited itself to a historical view of its problems."[44]

The Council's pronouncement, while giving official sanction to a more active involvement in management services, did not define the scope of this area. In 1956 the Institute published a classification of Management Services by CPAs, which listed 116 items of service performed by at least one of 43 firms responding to a questionnaire pertaining to this area.[45] While some of the items were classified in the category of production, marketing and personnel, the "overwhelming preponderance of services which these thirty-three firms had performed fell in the area of finance and control.[46] Included in this area were such services as forecasts of capital expenditure needs, working capital requirements and money market conditions; tax minimization; administration of pension and similar funds; planning and budgeting; and systems and procedures.[47] In 1962, a survey of smaller CPA firms conducted by the Institute "indicated that most management services are being rendered by CPAs in the areas of general management, internal and external reporting, costs, budgeting, systems and data processing."[48]

Defining the contents of the management services function is argued as necessary by some and unnecessary by others. The "expansionists" imply that the practitioner, so long as he is proficient to do so, may perform any service for management which does not breach the confines of other professions. They would include such client services as planning organizational objectives and personnel recruitment. In effect, they favor an almost limitless boundary to the management services function.

The present study accepts a contrary view of the scope of management services. It is based on the idea that "professional consulting, as distinguished from personal advice, is properly performed only in relation to a structured body of knowledge, where it is possible to review consulting advice of an objective basis."[49] The scope of the management services function is considered to be affected by the changing role of the controller, management's internally-located information specialist. It is assumed that this role has expanded from one where primary regard was for financially-oriented information and control to one where concern is for all information and techniques necessary for overall planning and control. It is further assumed that the boundaries of this role are determinable. Therefore, the management services function is concerned with all phases of the management information system, "which has to do with the entire process of quantitative information gathering, inclusive of the accounting function but not limited to it."[50] All the traditional tools and techniques of the accountant are included here, such as budgets, standard costs and forecasts; however, newer tools and techniques are also incorporated and coordinated with the traditional ones.

In order to perform the management services role effectively, CPAs must be well informed on the theoretical subject matter of the entire field of accounting and of related disciplines. Furthermore, they must be able to integrate accounting with these disciplines while solving the practical problems confronting clients. They must be familiar with the existing state of computer technology and all new developments which affect the management services function. CPAs must also be able to incorporate these into systems concepts and applications. Only in this way will the public accounting profession maintain the special place it now enjoys when the era of information technology becomes a complete reality. Like it or not, the transition to that era is under way.

III

The Data-Processing Service Bureau

During the past year, existing management information systems
have begun to resemble those predicted in the technical literature of
preceding years.[1] For the CPA engaged in management services
activities, there is an ever-increasing stream of client requests for the
installation or modification of existing information and control systems. Many of these requests convey expectations of computerized
systems. The expectations stem from an awareness of the existence
of versatile and flexible computers, ranging from highly sophisticated
desk models to large computers capable of accommodating many
different firms. Clients recognize that automated data processing,
storage, and retrieval are feasible for firms of practically every size.
Many clients further realize that the day for automating only the
clerically oriented operations, such as payroll, has ended. Consequently, the CPA faces not only more numerous requests, but requests
which indicate information is receiving recognition as an important
resource, sharing equal status with the factors of production.

In this chapter, data-processing service bureaus, potential components of management information systems, are examined. First,
a group of general considerations relating to the service bureau industry are explored. Then the different types of service bureaus are
described, differentiated by ownership and service specialty. Finally,
a typical service bureau organizational structure and method of operation are considered.

SERVICE BUREAUS: SOME GENERAL CONSIDERATIONS

In order to appreciate the potential capabilities of service bureaus as information systems aids, it may be useful to consider the industry, to trace the history of service bureaus, to examine some industry financial statistics, to review the role of the industry trade association, and to describe certain problem areas confronting service bureaus.

The Service Bureau Industry

The service bureau industry is composed of fee-charging organizations which offer a wide range of data-processing services to customers on an as-needed and contract basis. The services offered are broadly categorized as machine-time rental, data processing, programming, and problem solving. An organization may offer a complete line of services or any combination thereof. Relatively few offer a complete line. Services are provided by various combinations of personnel and equipment, the combination employed being dictated by the nature of an engagement.

For the purpose of this study, the broadest possible definition of a service bureau is adopted:

Service bureaus come in almost every shape and size. Some have lots of equipment, some have none; some specialize in particular applications, some will tackle almost anything; some operate nationally, others locally; some have hundreds of employees, some have only one; some are run by equipment manufacturers, some are independent. . . . The contrasts and diversities of the industry are too numerous to list, but the one thing all service bureaus have in common is that they each perform some type of data processing service on a fee basis.[2]

This definition is broad enough to include the computer services firms, i.e., the "software houses," firms specializing exclusively in the development of computer systems and programs, and the "problem solvers," firms undertaking only those projects requiring great imagination, creativity, and foresight. The latter group of firms usually develops a complex computer system or program as the end product of a project or they may use the computer only as a means for deriving a project's solution. Some computer services firms offer these services in conjunction with conventional data-processing assistance. Usually, if a firm offers services in addition to problem-solving assistance, it will be a "full line house," offering data processing and programming assistance. For the purposes of this study, organizationally independent data-processing installations operated by accounting firms, banks, foundations, universities, and other enterprises typically not considered a part of the data-processing industry are assumed to be service bureaus if they offer services to outside parties of a type and on a basis as those offered by conventional service bureaus.

Personnel employed. The personnel employed in the service bureau industry are its most important asset. Leonard J. Palmer notes that "the equipment is already more capable than most of the people in private organizations know how to utilize."[3] He further adds, "of all significant factors that go into a service bureau organization makeup, I would say hardware is the least significant. . . . I have told equipment manufacturers that they can give me the worst computer in an organization and the best people and I will compete with anybody."[4]

The skill levels of the personnel employed range from those required to operate equipment to those necessary for solving problems requiring originality and imagination. In terms of background, a service bureau studied by a leading technical periodical had, besides personnel capable of operating the equipment and writing the programs, "a Ph.D. in Chemical Engineering, specialists in accounting and inventory control, marketing specialists, top level mathematicians, including Fortran specialists, an operations research expert, civil engineers with outstanding achievements in PERT cost systems development, information retrieval specialists, etc."[5] Certain firms in this category have earned the name of "think factories."[6] The advantage to the user of such services or of the less sophisticated services is that he pays for only those which he needs and uses. More important, he is spared the problem of obtaining and retaining high-priced personnel.

Equipment utilized. The service bureau industry prides itself on the quality of its equipment, ranging from basic tabulating machines to highly sophisticated configurations of the most powerful computers available.

The type of equipment utilized affects the variety of applications offered, certainly in terms of economic feasibility. For example, analytical applications which may take seconds to process on a computer could take hours to process on tabulating equipment. A production control application which sets up the shop operating plan for each ensuing day could be run on tabulating equipment. However, the complexity of such an application requires many passes through the equipment before the solution becomes available. A computer provides a solution in a fraction of the time.

It is interesting to note that some service bureaus do not operate their own equipment. Such firms concentrate on programming or problem solving and may rent time at an off-premise location or contract the precessing portion of a project to another service bureau. Even without equipment, these firms can be considered service bureaus because of the staff employed. On the other hand, a number of banks too small to own their own data processing installations often offer service bureau-type services to customers. These banks either have an automated correspondent bank perform this work or they contract it to a service bureau. While such organizations may consider themselves a part of the service bureau industry, they are excluded because they do not employ the required staff. In addition, some less reputable firms and individuals offer data-processing services from time to time without utilizing their own equipment. Their customer's work is either contracted to a service bureau or run on an employer's equipment, often after business hours. Again, such operations are not considered service bureaus.

Number of firms in the industry. It has been estimated that some 1,200 computerized commercial service bureaus operate in the United States and Canada, counting each office of a multi-office firm separately and including in this count some of the offices of multi-office firms which operate large-scale tabulating installations.[7] The numerous smaller tabulating installations which proliferate within the industry and the fee-charging computer centers of CPA firms, banks, business firms, universities, and foundations magnify that number many times over.

Historical Sketch of the Industry

The service bureau industry reflects a degree of specialization characteristic of our economy. In order to compete successfully a firm must have access to the technological advances available to its industry. Larger firms create new positions or whole departments to reflect the specialized knowledge content of new developments. Smaller firms are not as fortunate. In terms of equipment, there is a point beyond which the smaller firm cannot progress, usually because of financial considerations. Furthermore, requiring existing personnel to master new techniques while continuing to perform their present duties places great limitations on their overall effectiveness. Consequently, smaller firms are forced to turn to outside service organizations in order to remain competitive. Larger firms frequently use outside service organizations also. One of their primary reasons is the competence of service organization personnel: another is the relative performance costs.

The data-processing service bureau concept had its origin in the services offered by scribes in the days of the ancient Egyptians and Hebrews.[8] Scribes performed their tallying and recording services, primitive forms of data processing, on a fee basis for various parties. Their skills, not commonly possessed, were in demand. Somilar skills, although greater in scope, attained new heights during the Middle Ages in certain northern Italian city-states. In feudal England, data processing services were further refined, as evidenced by the bookkeeping techniques of stewards. In the late nineteenth century, English public stenographers were offering their special data processing services.[9] The pressures of the Industrial Revolution found firms demanding these services because they were either unable or unwilling to provide their own. Organizations were soon formed to provide such specialized services because the demand was too great for individuals to provide them singly.

In the United States during the 1930's, temporary office services appeared for the purpose of supplying peak load personnel for office work and substitutes for vacationing or ill employees. The development of this concept and its effects on the service bureau industry were described as follows:

Occasionally, the peak load assignments required equipment as well as people. Among the first assignments was the extension of inventory tallies, for which full keyboard calculating machines were especially useful. During World War II this equipment, as well as office personnel, was in great demand. This circumstance accelerated the growth and acceptance of temporary help and service organizations in general. Again World War II witnessed an unprecedented demand for office space, whereupon source material was sent to the office of the supplier of temporary help for handling on his premises. Thus, along with personnel and equipment, space was made available to clients, and the data processing service center came into being.[10]

The growth of data-processing service organizations was not limited solely to advances in the techniques employed by individuals and organizations offering such services. Important advances in equipment occurred. Notched sticks, knotted strings, and the abacus were followed by Pascal's number wheel and ratchet, Babbage's analytical engine, and Thomas' forerunner of the modern desk calculator. During the decade 1880-1890, Hollerith and Powers developed punched card equipment capable of processing great volumes of data.[11] With ensuing advances, such equipment became commercially available early in the twentieth century.

In 1932, the International Business Machines Corporation (IBM) initiated a service offering punched card equipment to an individual, organization, or business on a hourly or job rental basis.[12] During the depression, many firms which had previously used their own equipment could no longer do so profitably. A great number of these firms found that they had to cancel their equipment leases with IBM. Hence it appears that IBM inaugurated the idea of a service bureau in part as a defensive measure. Of the firms which had previously justified economically the on-premises use of such equipment but which no longer could do so because of the depression, many found they could afford to rent a few hours of machine time per week.[13] In addition, many firms which could not justify leasing equipment before the depression found such equipment within their means for the first time.[14] By then, ". . . the functions of supplying temporary office help and of rendering data processing service became recognized as distinct activities—a distinction which was completed irrevocably by the introduction of the computer and its peripheral devices, and by legislative restrictions involving the temporary help supply companies."[15]

For approximately the next two decades, the development of the service bureau industry was inextricably entwined with the history of IBM.[16] In 1948, IBM installed a Selective Sequence Electronic Calculator in their New York City service bureau.[17] This was the first specialized equipment to be furnished on a off-premises rental basis. In 1952, IBM installed a 701 electronic digital computer in their New York service bureau. This computer was used for certain business-oriented applications such as refinery production planning.

Until the early 1960's, IBM had a near-monopoly upon the industry through its wholly-owned subsidiary, the Service Bureau Corporation (SBC), created in 1957. However, other computer manufacturers and independent firms have entered the industry and changed the competitive climate. The more recent emergence of bank computer centers as providers of service bureau-type services is changing that climate even more. Added to this, the types of services offered have changed drastically in importance since the inception of the service bureau concept. Today, machine-time rental is a very small segment of the services rendered. Services requiring skilled personnel have assumed the dominant role. Finally, just as the demands of the industrial revolution "forced the concentration of capital, equipment and personnel into new and large industrial enterprises and emphasized specialization, in a similar manner, the introduction of the computer into office work has forced the concentration of capital and equipment into specialty offices—the service centers."[18] And as the true potential of the computer is appreciated, the importance of skilled personnel to propel the computer's uses beyond the office and into the whole of the firm is recognized. It is in this last application that the modern service bureau has the most to offer.

Financial Aspects of the Industry

As noted, the services rendered by the service bureau industry fall into four major categories. Ranked in an ascending order of the degree of sophistication involved in their performance, these services are machine-time renting, data processing, programming assistance, and problem solving. The market for them represents a billion dollar business.[19] Annual expenditures for these services have been representing approximately 30 percent of all types of expenditures made in the electronic data processing market, which also includes leases and purchases of computers and peripheral equipment. In 1964, total expenditures in the electronic data-processing market approached $5.75 billion; by 1970 they are projected at $9.4 billion.[20] However, the rate of increase in expenditures for services only will be greater than that for aggregate electronic data processing expenditures by 1970, accounting for $3 billion.[21]

It should be noted that the service bureau industry does not receive all of the revenues from data processing services. Eighty percent or more of these service revenues are captured by the equipment manufacturers.[22] In addition, of the remaining 20 percent, estimated at $350 million in 1965 and projected at $700 million in 1970, the computer manufacturers receive their share through their service bureau subsidiaries or divisions.[23] IBM, Sperry Rand, General Electric, Radio Corporation of America, National Cash Register, and Honeywell fall into this category. However, publicly held independent service bureaus such as C-E-I-R, Computer Sciences Corporation, Planning Research Corporation, Computer Usage Corporation and Computer Applications together grossed some $50 million in 1964 and may have approached $100 million in 1965.[24] In comparison, the Service Bureau Corporation, IBM's subsidiary, was believed to have had a volume of $70 million in 1964.[25]

There are several factors which account for the spectacular growth of the service bureau industry. Among these factors is the introduction of second and third generation computers, operating in an on-line real-time mode with high speed communications and random-access storage, which have transformed the computer into the catalyst for a "true management information system." However, a firm cannot make the transition to a true management information system without innovations in operating methods. These innovations require skilled personnel. But the reservoir of available personnel has been drained due to the personnel requirements imposed by the spectacular computer investments of the past few years.[26] A second factor accounting for the spectacular growth of the industry is that many skilled personnel often prefer employment with a service bureau. In addition, the computer manufacturers are already experiencing a "software gap," finding it increasingly difficult to fulfill their software obligations. This factor makes the manufacturers very good customers of service bureaus and assures the growth of the service bureau industry.

The Industry Trade Association

The Association of Data Processing Service Organizations, which uses the acronym ADAPSO, is the service bureau industry's trade association. ADAPSO, founded in June of 1960, seeks promotion of service bureau usage throughout the United States and Canada.[27] In order to meet the expanding demand for professional data-processing services, it is felt that such an organization will act as a catalyst for information and idea exchange between service bureaus. Broader uses of facilities, new concepts in applications, and fresh approaches to problem solving are some of the anticipated benefits from membership in the organization. The first president of ADAPSO enunciated the following as the organization's initial aim:

As owners, managers and executives of data processing service companies, we will continually advance the art of rendering such services by stimulating the development of data processing techniques and thus promote data processing in general.[28]

The objectives of the organization are as follows:

The Association shall direct its efforts toward the improvement of management methods and service possibilities; the development of an appreciation for high ethical and performance standards; and the creation of an atmosphere of general public acceptance for data processing services.[29]

ADAPSO, whose membership numbered an even 100 as of March of 1965, employs the following definitions as criteria for membership:

Experienced operating centers whose major interest is that of performing data processing for a number of outside clients, for profit, while regularly utilizing data processing facilities in such a manner that physical control of, and working responsibility for, the chain of processing steps is maintained by, and prime responsibility for completed results rests with, the bureau.

Experienced, formally established, identifiable and self-contained data processing units of general purpose enterprises, provided the major interest of the data processing unit is that of performing data processing for a number of outside clients, for profit, while regularly utilizing data processing facilities in such a manner that physical control of, and working responsibility for, the chain of processing steps is maintained by, and prime responsibility for completed results rests with, the bureau.[30]

The definitions stress that a service bureau's major interest should be that of providing service to a number of outside customers and not existing primarily to further the interests of a parent company. The words "for profit" are noteworthy in that they exclude organizations primarily interested in research, experimentation, or training. Finally, the phrases "physical control of," and "working responsibility for," exclude from membership firms which act as brokers in that they gather and sublet data-processing work. Members must perform the work on their premises, utilizing the standard service bureau equipment such as "punched cards, punched and magnetic tapes, optical readers, computers and related pieces."[31] It should be noted that within the definitions which establish the criteria for membership, data processing does not, of necessity, involve the use of computers.

A Descriptive Summary of the
Different Types of Service Bureaus

Service bureaus are here differentiated and described on the basis of ownership and service specialty. Of course, a single firm will ordinarily be categorized under both groupings. Furthermore, the two groupings selected are not the only feasible ones: e.g., service bureaus can also be differentiated on the basis of equipment utilized.

Differentiation by Ownership

Service bureau ownership falls into the following major groups:
1. computer manufacturer's divisions or subsidiaries
2. independently owned service bureaus
3. departments of commercial banks or bank computer cooperatives
4. computer centers of CPA firms or CPA computer cooperatives
5. various miscellaneous groupings

Each is described in turn.

Computer manufacturers' divisions or subsidiaries. Computer manufacturers find the operation of their own service bureaus a logical extension of their equipment sales activities. In the first place, service bureaus provide the manufacturer a place to put equipment to work earning at least the equivalent of a lease payment. Further, their parent companies do not consider them loss-leaders. Another advantage accruing to the computer manufacturer is that the service bureau serves as an effective means of sales promotion. A potential customer can observe, in operation, the type of equipment he contemplates purchasing. In addition, he can bring his personnel to the service bureau for training in the operation of such equipment prior to its installation. Many firms find manufacturers' service bureaus effective aids in adopting computerized systems or in modifying existing systems. The advantages to this approach are obvious. Precious capital is conserved if it is determined that the computer will not function satisfactorily and large benefits accrue if the transition to a new system can take place efficiently.

Independently owned service bureaus. These are generally closely held companies. Often there is a great disparity in the level of sophistication between the larger and smaller organizations in this category. The larger firms are often very scientific and research oriented while the smaller ones have a more commercial or business orientation. For example, the largest of the publicly-held service bureaus, C-E-I-R, now a Control Data Corporation subsidiary, was conceived by a group of top-level scientists, statisticians, and mathematicians formerly employed by the Defense Department. While C-E-I-R provides commercially oriented services, it is best known for its scientific and research programming and problem solving. Similarly, Computer Sciences Corporation (CSC) in El Segundo, California, prefers to assist computer owners in realizing the benefits of the complex technological aspects of data processing. CSC markets such things as an information-retrieval system for managing personnel records and a group of programs for handling stock certificate transfers. In addition, the acquisition of two subsidiaries of International Telephone and Telegraph places CSC in the business of developing software sub-systems for the Telstar II communications satellite. Furthermore, large independent firms often are the designers of new software systems introduced by the computer manufacturers. In fact, the computer manufacturers are among their best clients.

The majority of independently owned service bureaus are not in the computer services or contract service part of the industry. While providing both programming assistance and processing services, their emphasis is usually on the latter. This is especially true of the firms using tabulating equipment. Their processing services very often consist mainly of sales analysis, billing, payroll, and financial statement preparation. Independently owned service bureaus using computers usually offer these services and rather sophisticated analyses and control applications in the areas of inventory and production. Many in this latter group also offer excellent systems and programming assistance.

Commercial banks. Commercial banks are rather recent entrants into the service bureau industry. Through their electronic data processing departments or divisions and their computer cooperatives, they have followed an interesting pattern of development.

In the 1950's the paper-handling problems of banks became acute. Between 1950 and 1960, the number of checking accounts rose 40 percent and the number of checks processed increased 75 percent.[32] In comparison, the increase in paper work was matched by only a 37 percent increase in demand-deposit dollar value.[33] Due to the fact that approximately one-half of all bank employees perform work associated with demand-deposit processing, the nation's banks found themselves in a profit squeeze. Automated data processing was selected as an answer to this problem by many banks.

Soon, a number of banks that obtained equipment found they had excess computer capacity. In fact, computers were often idle during the working day because most transactions were processed after closing hours. In order to utilize some of their excess capacity, banks with on-premises computers began offering the internal computer applications they were processing for themselves to their correspondents. This is still an important segment of their computer services sales. The next step for these banks was to handle bookkeeping for other financial institutions such as Savings and Loan Associations and systematic savings accounts for mutual funds.

Now, the real drive by banks is to sell computer services to customers— chiefly corporate customers but also some individuals. The aim, increasingly, is not just to fill idle computer time, but to develop new deposits and make the computer a generator of profits on its own.[34]

The impact of banks upon the accounting profession will be discussed in more detail in a subsequent chapter. For now, it is sufficient to note that their computer services are generally associated with business-oriented processing, some programming assistance, and virtually no high-level problem solving.

CPA computer installations. The AICPA recently reported that at least 100 of its member firms had acquired a computer, and that at least 55 member firms were using another CPA firm's equipment to service clients.[35] A survey by the Michigan Association of Certified Public Accountants in March of 1966 found that at least 11 member firms either operate their own automated data-processing equipment for servicing clients or have a financial interest in such an installation.[36] Compared to the size of the service bureau industry and the activities of banks rendering computerized customer services, these statistics seem insignificant. When the efforts of these CPA firms are examined in the context of the profession's ethical philosophy and its traditional conservatism, these statistics are important. They represent a positive approach toward meeting the challenges of information technology and the electronic computer. Unfortunately, the ethical status of such an approach has not as yet been fully resolved by the profession. As in many other areas, the profession has adopted a dangerous wait-and-see posture supported only by the research of the AICPA in conjunction with the System Development Corporation.

The New York firm of Lennox and Lennox is an example of an exceptionally strong commitment to the operation of a computer installation. This CPA firm entered the automated data-processing field in 1958 with an add-punch, which is basically a punched paper tape-producing device usually connected to an adding machine. John Lennox noted:

Our initial exposure was gained via the use of a commercial service bureau where a simple, non-flexible, financial statement format was used to produce statements for our clients. This service bureau served a purpose in those days, but we, in our firm, soon recognized that they were not accountants and so did not understand the needs of accountants to satisfy, in turn, their clients' needs.[37]

In time, the firm substituted an NCR 3100 Accounting Machine for the add-punch. Soon, the firm's records were maintained on the NCR bookkeeping machine, which also produced a punched paper tape. In addition, the staff was gaining valuable experience in the field of automated data processing. By 1961, partially in response to the increased demand of clients for budgets, budget comparisons, detailed analyses, and special statements, the firm acquired an NCR 390 computer.

With the acquisition of the NCR 390, the firm developed 33 accountant-type programs which fitted a variety of its own clients' needs. Soon, Lennox and Lennox received requests from other CPA firms wishing to have their clients' data processed by these programs. Added to this, referral requests from other CPAs for electronic data processing feasibility studies and systems design and installation studies were received. At this point, Lennox and Lennox concurrently formed an accounting service bureau and a management services division. Recently the firm was engaged by the National Retail Merchants Association to devise a complete system for the Association's members. Lennox and Lennox now have a six-year contract to process, for the Association's members, the reports designed into this system.

Other types of service bureaus. Universities and foundations renting free time on computers which are primarily maintained to service their needs are beyond the scope of this study. They are of negligible importance in terms of commercial or business-oriented applications; however, several are quite important in scientific work for industry and government. Firms renting time on their computer installations are not service bureaus in any sense of the word because they generally are not staffed to serve, nor do they actively solicit, outside clients. They usually perform limited processing services on an irregular basis.

Certain large firms maintain data-processing centers as separate divisions or subsidiaries. These service bureaus assist outside firms and consider the parent almost as another outsider. One of the largest of such installations is McDonnel Aircraft Corporation's Automation Center. The main installation is in St. Louis, with additional facilities in Denver, Houston, and Columbia, Missouri. In total, the McDonnell Automation Center has upwards of $20 million dollars of conventional punched card, digital and analog equipment, and it employs about 800 people.[38] Its services include problem definition, consulting, systems design, program construction, and data processing. Customers range in size from very small firms to industrial giants, and they are engaged in such businesses as advertising, accounting, brewing, finance, banking, petroleum engineering, and uranium processing. Specific commercial processing services include labor and material costing, financial status forecasting, development of production schedules, and advertising research. Scientific services include analysis of variance, matrix calculations, and flutter and stress analysis.

Service Bureaus Differentiated by Service Specialty

The differentiation of service bureaus by service specialty is perhaps the most meaningful and useful method of examining them. Yet it is very difficult to classify some firms into only one category. However, for purposes of analysis, it will be assumed that such a task can be accomplished. The types of firms described are equipment-time renters, accountants'-program specialists, federal income tax processers, industry specialists, the problem solvers, the full-line houses, and a miscellaneous group.

Equipment-time renters. In 1959, IBM, in partial competition with its wholly-owned subsidiary, the Service Bureau Corporation, inaugurated a chain of service bureaus where customers rent computer time and process their own work with their own personnel. In 1965, the Statistical Tabulating Corporation (STC) opened, in Chicago, its first Data-Mat, a do-it-yourself service bureau which allows customers to drive in and process data much as a housewife drives to a laundromat to do the family wash. Basically these services enable customers to bring their unprocessed data to a mid-town service bureau, to park free of charge, to use the facilities of a private office while organizing the unprocessed data, and to process the data on new high-speed computer systems. Even permanent storage facilities are provided. These data centers ordinarily operate 24 hours a day, 7 days a week, with trained personnel available at all times to render assistance.

STC estimated that some 2,000 local Chicago firms are potential users of Data-Mat, which in effect permits these firms to own some fraction of a computer's total capabilities. Most of these firms are small retail, finance, banking, service, and manufacturing businesses whose volume does not justify an on-premises installation. Another potential market is among firms with their own on-premises equipment who have periodic peak-load requirements. As of 1965, Illinois Bell, Morton Salt, and Standard Brands had contracted for services.

One of the primary aims of Data-Mat is to provide services for firms in the transition stage between using a conventional service bureau, i.e., one that performs the entire job for a customer, and maintaining its own on-premises computer installation. The computer cost and its related investment and maintenance outlays are borne by the service bureau. The customer provides his personnel, who gain valuable experience, and concurrently uses the service bureau as a proving ground for a planned on-premises installation.

Accountants'-program specialists. Some service bureaus specialize in offering programs attractive to an accountant serving a group of relatively small clients. A survey of the literature on service bureaus reveals this type to be the most frequently described. Such a situation is unfortunate because it reinforces a basic misconception shared by most CPAs as to the potential of data-processing service bureaus and of the electronic computer. It further fosters a very narrow understanding of the larger field of information technology. Examples of unimaginative uses of service bureaus superimposed on outmoded systems are common. Each example further raises questions as to the CPA's competence as a provider of managerial information. Literature extolling the merits of such inadequate installations are examples of delusion. The accountant is in effect being told what he wishes to hear. He is assured that his old ways of doing things will not be affected by service bureau applications. Any efforts necessary for him to acquire new talents are minimized.

Service bureaus specializing in accountants' programs generally do so through the use of "package" programs, capable of processing the data of a relatively wide range of firms. However, modifications in the existing chart of accounts and other relatively minor systems changes usually must be made before a firm's data can be processed. The most common type of package program prepares the financial statements, updates the general ledger, and details the changes which occurred in each account during an accounting period. In effect, the write-up work so prevalent among smaller practitioners is now automated.

It is characteristic of accountants'-program specialists to deal through the accountant under ordinary circumstances. The accountant sends the raw data to the service bureau and receives the financial statements and the updated general ledger. One of the leading independently owned service bureaus in this field emphasizes that absolute control is in the accountant's hands. All that is required is some means of getting the raw data to the service bureau. This is often in the form of punched paper tape or microfilmed source documents. The accountant then presents the records to his client. Various governmental compliance reports and payroll processing, to include withholding statements, are often prepared. The more sophisticated service bureaus specializing in accountants' programs offer various analyses and control applications. Some even offer custom designed programs.

Federal income tax return processing services. The computer processing of individual federal income tax returns and the individual tax returns in certain states has been available to CPAs during the past few years. Such services are carried out through certain organizations which contract portions of the processing to established service bureaus. There are no service bureaus, as such, specializing exclusively in tax returns. The originator of computer-prepared income tax returns is Computer Sciences Corporation. In 1965, Computer Sciences sold over 50 percent of its interest in the Computax System to Commerce Clearing House. There are several other entrants into this field, among them Monroe Data Processing's Datatax.

The mechanics of the Computax system are fairly simple. First, the CPA enters the necessary information on specially designed input forms. These are similar to the preprinted audit worksheets and schedules used by many CPA firms. The forms are sent to Computax Corporation, where key-punch operators transform the data into machine-sensible media. The media are then processed by the computer and the completed tax returns are returned to the CPA. Of course, this service is somewhat limited in its flexibility: for example, in areas requiring judgment. However, most calculations are very efficiently processed by the computer. Some of the other benefits ascribed to this system are checking the returns for missing or inconsistent information, revealing areas for potential tax deduction, and relieving the accountant of many clerical procedures.[39]

It is expected that computerized tax services will be expanded to include such activities as preparing corporate, estate and partnership returns, checking dividend income and security transactions, year-end tax reviews, determining tax advantages of the corporate vs. the partnership form of doing business, estate planning, and information retrieval of tax court decisions.[40]

Industry specialists. Probably the biggest cost associated with data processing is that of program development. Programming costs can easily run into the tens of thousands of dollars; and many times the initial programming cost for a custom-designed program will exceed the first year's revenue from processing the associated data.[41] Therefore, if a market potential for a particular application exists, it is wise for service bureaus to consider developing a package program for that application. In this way, the various costs of program development are recovered more quickly from a number of users. In addition, there are several other advantages of package programs. From the point of view of the service bureau, programmers' efforts can be applied to many areas, and customers using package programs represent a relatively stable base of repeat processing business. Future alterations in a package program due to an application's changed requirements can be undertaken easily, in comparison with modifying several separate custom-designed programs. For the customer, the use of a package program is clearly less expensive than the use of a custom-designed program. However, the customer must often accept a certain degree of inflexibility when using a package program. To counteract this, some service bureaus offer flexible package programs with parts that can be modified.[42] Such a program is more difficult to develop, requires high-level personnel to design, and may be more difficult to process. But it is easier to market because of its flexibility.

Partially due to the advantages of package programs, service bureaus have emerged specializing in applications peculiar to a particular industry. By concentrating their efforts on an industry, these organizations are able to develop very efficient package programs. They are also able to mass the talents of their systems and programming personnel for developing future applications. Such applications are easily determined through the service bureau's intimate knowledge of a particular industry, and the inflexibility inherent in a package program is, at the same time, mitigated. The type of application varies from one industry to another. "For example, invoicing in a lumber yard with its complex discounting and credit problems is not the same as invoicing in a tool and die shop."[43] Learning this lesson, some service bureaus have put together several applications peculiar to the needs of an industry and now offer what amounts to a system package for it. Hospitals, truckers, form printers and automobile dealers are some of the lines of business served by these specialized service bureaus.[44]

Reynolds and Reynolds is an example of a service bureau specializing in a package system for automobile dealers. Starting with a few local Ohio dealers in 1963, they had expanded nationally to over 1000 dealers in 1965.[45] The system is based on some well-designed source document forms peculiar to an automobile dealer's requirements. The information on the form is reproduced by an add-punch into punched paper tape or by a special adding machine onto printed tape readable by machines and humans alike. The tape is mailed daily to the service bureau. In turn, the service bureau produces operating controls daily, customer statements on the 25th of each month, and detail journals and a general ledger monthly.

Problem solvers. Service bureaus classified as problem solvers or "think factories" represent the most exotic and dynamic part of the industry. Some of them do not operate their own equipment, or hardware, but prefer to rent computer time as they need it. Such an attitude of considering machines second to human talent is successful in attracting talent. It appears that aside from financial rewards, a professional would rather work among fellow professionals. Within organizations of this type, the professional is in the mainstream and he is not a staff specialist located in some organizationally remote section. From the standpoint of financial rewards, compensation is often greater with consulting-oriented service bureaus because most firms cannot afford to maintain such an array of talent. However, a great many firms can afford the expense of having special problems solved by true professionals.

The problems these think factories can solve know practically no boundaries. Many disciplines such as operations research, economics, econometrics, mathematics, and statistics are employed in order to seek solutions to a full spectrum of scientific and commercial applications. The following are examples of the capabilities of C-E-I-R, one of the largest of the problem solvers:

1. For the oil industry, C-E-I-R has helped in the development, engineering and running of systems to assist top oil executives in scheduling refining, transportation, and distribution within their complex of refineries, tanker fleets, and distribution systems.

2. For the tobacco industry, C-E-I-R completed a comprehensive study showing the impact of the industry upon other sectors of the economy in all 50 states. With this study, the tobacco industry was able to trace the contribution of tobacco sales to personal consumption, employment, worker income and tax revenues.

3. For the Defense Department, C-E-I-R performed an analytical and statistical study, by industry and by geographic area, of the impact of defense expenditures on the economy. In addition, C-E-I-R is providing continued support in the form of a large-scale statistical reliability study for the Polaris program.

4. C-E-I-R economists, market research analysts, and statisticians have worked closely with many city planning bodies, private investment groups, and transportation agencies concerned with metropolitan area problems. In conjunction with this, C-E-I-R has projected the size and composition of a major metropolitan area's population and economy and the related mass transportation problems 10 to 25 years into the future.

5. C-E-I-R has made major progress toward developing compilers which will allow any technical expert to address a computer in the language of his own expertise, stating his problems as he prefers to state them, and concentrating on obtaining a solution without attention to computer housekeeping and other extraneous factors.

6. C-E-I-R has a unique corps of statistical and data experts to assist clients in mobilizing appropriate data, and in designing statistical and accounting reporting systems for meaningful data processing.[46]

Full-line houses. Service bureaus referred to as "full-line" houses offer a wide range of services. However, relatively few offer the complete spectrum of services discussed earlier in this chapter; there are great differences between them in the degree of emphasis placed and expertise demonstrated in each type of service. Many full-line houses are often referred to as conventional service bureaus, in that the services rendered, such as systems and program design and data processing, are those most commonly ascribed to service bureaus. Conventional service bureaus usually do not undertake sophisticated problem-solving projects nor do they specialize in applications peculiar to specific industries. Individual federal income tax return preparation is similarly not offered. However, such service bureaus may offer some specialized industry systems, accountant's packages, billing, payroll, inventory, production control, and a host of other applications.

Other categories. In addition to the major types of service bureaus differentiated by services rendered, there are some offering very specialized services, often in areas wholly unrelated to service bureau operations as described. For example, Computer Sciences Corporation manufactures special items of electronic equipment. C-E-I-R once owned Automation Institute of America, the oldest and largest organization offering training in the basic skills of business automation. In addition, C-E-I-R franchises service bureaus. Computer Usage Corporation, basically a problem solver and programming specialist boasting a large part of its volume from computer manufacturers, has made a name for itself in the machine-time brokerage business. The firm rents the available computer time of other companies, fits them together into an overall schedule and subleases the time to its clients.

A West Coast service bureau offers a central credit reference service. It classifies individuals by driver's license number and obtains credit data related to them. A merchant subscribing to this service receives rapid credit information simply by telephoning the service bureau. In Ohio, a service bureau offers a complete traffic billing service with which transportation companies clear accounts with one another and pay all monthly bills with a single check. It also aids in planning shipping routes, modes of shipment, etc. Another service bureau provides a service whereby home builders submit their project plans for comparison with an experience file of other builders. A detailed critique is then prepared of the proposed plan. Other service bureaus aid customers by assisting them in selecting their own on-premises computer installations once such a move is deemed advantageous.

A relative newcomer is the information or microfilm service bureau, which stores documents on microfilm and retrieves and reproduces them upon a customer's request. "The customer is provided with statistical and accounting reports, answers to specific or general requests, and organized files."[47] Often, these service bureaus specialize in a particular industry. For example, one such organization provides information on patient care and treatment methods for hospitals, while another supplies emergency drug information for medical doctor subscribers. A third provides a mechanized purchasing and procurement catalog file for the electronics and aero-space industries. Special equipment installed at each subscriber's location permits an engineer or purchasing agent to view microfilmed catalog pages of all companies supplying a particular product. When the desired product is selected, a listing of all of the vendors' sales and engineering offices can be flashed onto the viewing screen.

SERVICE BUREAU ORGANIZATION AND OPERATION

A description of the organization structure and operation of a conventional service bureau is presented here. The material is general in nature, applicable in varying degrees to service bureaus of all types.[48]

Service Bureau Organization Structure

The literature surveyed and the field interviews conducted suggest that a service bureau is usually organized along functional lines, resembling the organizational structure of a typical manufacturing firm. One exception is that the finance function does not share the importance of sales and production. While this may be surprising because of the high costs of computer and peripheral equipment and the salaries of skilled personnel, it can be readily explained in terms of a relatively smaller and less complex scale of operations, and an uncomplicated capital structure characteristic of many closely-held companies. However, the investment in equipment is more apparent than real. Many service bureaus lease their equipment. In addition, there are no sizeable inventories and, as in many service organizations, management tends to be either sales- or production-oriented.

Regardless of the size of a conventional service bureau, certain functions, including sales, systems and programming, and production, must be performed in order to attain acceptable operating standards. Usually, these functions constitute the first level of management below the president for service bureaus with gross revenues of over $300,000 per year.[49] For smaller service bureaus, the owner-manager will often manage all of these functions. In terms of staff functions, the most important is that associated with the research and development of software applications. Figure III-1 illustrates an organization structure appropriate for service bureaus with annual gross revenues over $1 million. This size is chosen for illustrative purposes in order that all functions and sub-functions can be represented separately.

The first function examined is sales. The sales manager's duties include market definition and customer acceptability. In order to penetrate or develop new markets and exploit existing ones, he conducts market research studies and recommends areas for the research and development of software package programs and systems. For acceptable customers, the sales manager prepares guidelines setting limits to sales efforts and developmental expenses. He assists the efforts of the sales force through training, advertising and promotional campaigns, and by reviewing the various proposals submitted by salesmen. Also, he evaluates the productivity of the sales effort. One of his most important duties is coordinating sales activities with those of the production department and the systems and programming department. With respect to the production department, the sales effort must consider the processing capacity and scheduled workload; and, in terms of the systems and programming department, the sales effort cannot exceed the available capacity expressed in terms of man-hours.

A West Coast service bureau has its sales department divided into two groups.[50] Sales representatives experienced in system design and analysis compose the first group. Their function is to acquaint customers with the service bureau's range of services and to analyze customer requirements and prepare solutions along with cost estimates. The second group, customer service representatives, call on existing customers and discuss any problems which may arise. They are also technically trained in operations and in systems and programming.

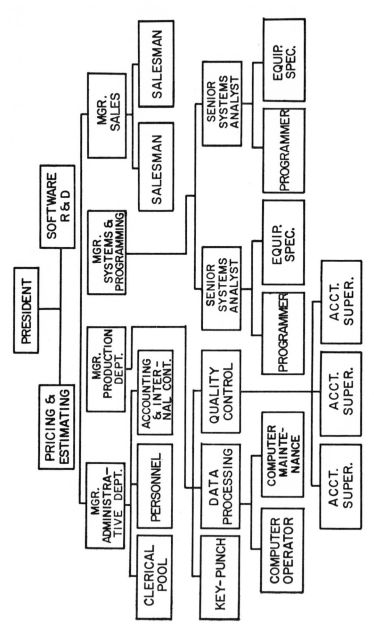

SERVICE BUREAU ORGANIZATIONAL STRUCTURE

FIGURE III-1

The systems and programming department manager defines the systems and program design concepts for all work processed by the service bureau. He defines and enforces standards for documenting programs and standardizing procedures. The latter step is important in the successful management of a service bureau.[51] All specifications submitted by the sales department are reviewed by the systems and programming department manager. He also exercises a degree of control over pricing and proposal techniques. Internally, he coordinates his activity with the sales manager, assigns projects to his work groups, and develops training programs, both formal and on-the-job, for his personnel. In addition, he supervises consulting services such as the design and installation of a customer's own computer system. Finally, he is responsible for the productivity of his senior systems analysts and their respective teams consisting of programmers and equipment specialists. These teams are the basic work group of the systems and programming department.

The production department is generally the largest department in a service bureau. Reporting to the production manager are the heads of the key-punch, quality-control, and data-processing sections. The key-punch section head is responsible for meeting the schedule requirements of his section by initiating and maintaining sound procedures which aid him in controlling closely the productivity of his section. Key-punch error detection and follow-up action are also his responsibility. The quality-control section chief is responsible for the control of customer records. The objectives of quality control are to reduce error conditions, and (because errors are bound to occur), to establish procedures for their correction. Therefore, the quality control section chief reviews all work processed, maintains control of recurring work through account supervisors, and promotes close liaison with customers at the operating level. The data-processing section chief is responsible for efficient computer utilization and productivity. It is the data-processing section head's duty to squeeze every second of running time out of the computer by skillful work scheduling, control and training of personnel, and equipment maintenance. The production department manager coordinates the duties of these sections among themselves and with the sales and systems and programming departments.

The staff functions common to most service bureaus of the size and type discussed are represented by the administrative, the software research and development, and the pricing and estimating departments. The first department may consist of a clerical pool, a personnel section, and an accounting or bookkeeping section. The normal housekeeping functions are conducted here. The second department, software research and development, is essential in giving an organization direction.[52] This department selects areas for applications which are potentially profitable and then designs the applications. By virtue of its role as a staff, it is shielded from the daily pressures faced by the systems and programming department. Consequently, it devotes its time to projects which profoundly influence the long-run well-being of the firm. The last department, pricing and estimating, is also quite important to the success of the firm. However, its objectives are more oriented to present benefits. While jobs can be added through sharp pricing and estimating policies, all costs and an adequate increment of profit must be recovered from total revenues for a firm to be successful. Effective pricing and estimating require a thorough understanding of this very critical function. Pricing policies cannot be too competitive or profits may suffer, and a firm may acquire an undesirable reputation with competitors and clients alike. Similarly, job estimating, especially with respect to program development, can degenerate to guesswork and can adversely affect pricing policies. Consequently, this department must be closely supervised by management.

Service Bureau Operations

Service bureau operations vary from firm to firm. The procedures described here are illustrative of the operations of a conventional one.

Contacts with prospective customers are generally made through the sales department. For prospects whose requirements are relatively uncomplicated, the sales representative provides the solution. Prospective package program users are an example of the type of applications a sales representative handles easily. Here, he is bound by guidelines set by the systems and programming department with respect to system design and by the guidelines established by the pricing and estimating department for price quotation purposes. Of course, the sales manager reviews the proposed application.

For highly complex customer requirements, such as for special or one-time jobs or for designing a customer's own equipment installation, a systems analyst is available. The analyst prepares the necessary system design complete with such documentation as programs, card layouts, flow charts, and reports.

When a prospect becomes a regular customer, his primary contact with the service bureau is usually through an account supervisor in the quality control section, which requests the support necessary to service recurring customers from the key punch and data-processing sections. The sales or systems and programming department also requests such support for one-time or special engagements and the software research department requests support for its developmental work.

Documents representing a customer's data to be processed arrive at the service bureau in various forms. The documents are received, logged in, and verified by a receiving unit under the control of the quality control section. Documents not in machine-sensible form are sent to the key punch section for conversion into punched cards. The punched cards are then forwarded to the data-processing section after various control procedures are carried out.

The data-processing section is usually divided into off-line and on-line areas. The off-line area is used to assemble and disassemble jobs. This step includes acquiring the client's permanent records from a security area and placing them in running order with the newly received data. The computer processing run up-dates the client's permanent records and simultaneously processes the new data into a desired form. In the on-line area, the proper program processes the data. After processing, the quality control section examines the permanent records and processed reports. At the completion of the job, the permanent records are returned to the security area and the reports are dispatched to the customer.

Control is maintained throughout the service bureau by a system of strict procedures which include log entries and various checks as documents move from one section to another. The logs can be compared to employee time reports completed by each operator showing the various jobs handled and the time involved. These reports serve a multiple purpose: they represent the basis for billing customers, for fixing responsibility upon employees, and for assuring optimal equipment utilization.

IV

The Certified Public Accountant, His Clients, and Service Bureaus

In this chapter, the potential working relationship between a CPA, his clients, and service bureaus is examined. Based on a review of the literature and personal interviews with CPAs and service bureaus actively working together, it is submitted that an informal working arrangement with a capable service bureau can materially benefit a CPA and his clients. Two general considerations and several possible approaches open to the CPA for working with service bureaus are examined to demonstrate this assertion. Then a description of a service bureau selection process and of the steps involved in preparing for a service bureau application illustrates the importance of planning in a succesful CPA, client, and service bureau relationship. The chapter concludes with a review of some of the possible advantages and disadvantages inherent in service bureau applications.

GENERAL CONSIDERATIONS

Prior to selecting a service bureau application as a part of a client's information system, the CPA should consider two factors. The first is that the use of service bureaus is but one automation alternative for a client's management information system. The second is that the CPA must build a working relationship between himself, clients, and service bureaus.

56

Service Bureaus as Alternative
Components in Systems Design

The existence of a material disparity between available and desired information is the signal to begin devising a means to bridge this gap. When the need for a new or modified information system develops, or the modification of an existing one is recognized, the CPA should examine the existing system in order that he may recognize alternative solutions to the problem.

The examination may indicate that relatively minor changes are necessary. Simply by re-assigning responsibilities, re-routing work flows, altering existing forms, adding or deleting reports, changing the office layout, or modifying clerical routines and procedures, the necessary information improvements are often obtained. All too frequently, however, poorly conceived proposals rush a client headlong into installing some form of automation when the problem is quite minor and easily corrected without incurring large expenditures. Even when the client does need some form of automation in his information system, the proposed solutions often go no further than the equipment purchase or lease consideration. Allowing for the increased capability and decreased cost of small computers, ownership still has many problems. For that matter, owning automated equipment of any type is not always the best solution to information inadequacies. Equipment cost is frequently a secondary factor; attracting and keeping qualified personnel is most critical. In addition, the equipment is often under-utilized in terms of processing time and of imaginative applications.

This study seeks to expand the number and sophistication of automation alternatives for clients' management information systems. It is submitted that data processing service bureaus represent a much more sophisticated alternative than CPAs generally recognize: service bureaus are not merely tools for automating write-up work. In this respect, CPAs are as guilty as many of their computer-owning clients who fail to utilize the computer's full potential. It is further submitted that service bureau relationships, wisely utilized, can increase the number of management services engagements just as legislation has increased audit and tax engagements. However, the CPA's rewards from EDP-related services often have a readily identifiable economic justification in the eyes of clients, certainly when compared with those derived from legislatively created audit and tax engagements.

The CPA-Client-Service Bureau Relationship

The client often relies upon his CPA for advice related to internal operations. A professionally motivated CPA welcomes this reliance and uses it as leverage allowing him to provide better services. For example, if a new technique can benefit a client, the CPA should use his influence to urge adoption of it. Of course, the CPA's recommendation would come after a careful study of the client's needs and the alternatives available to satisfy such needs.

The CPA's ability as an analyst often appears greater than his knowledge of advances in his field. The burden of daily requirements leaves little time, according to some practitioners, for evaluating new techniques. Then, too, some CPAs lack the ability to communicate effectively. In this case, although the CPA thoroughly studies a new technique and judges it beneficial to a client, he may be unable to convince the client.

The true professional manages to keep informed of those developments which best aid his clients. Professional associations and their journals regularly report new developments; however their coverage is often designed to orient and direct the reader rather than to train him. Hence, the professionally motivated practitioner must set aside time for independent research in order to deserve his clients' confidence.

Unfortunately, not all CPAs are professionally motivated to the extent that they keep pace with progress. The careful, conservative approach to solving clients' problems is often used as an excuse for inactivity in seeking to learn of newly emerging developments. CPAs of this type are largely responsible for the charges leveled against the profession about its slow reaction to a changing environment. These same CPAs are among the most complacent: content with employing yesterday's techniques for today's problems while totally disregarding the future. Yet clients continue to hold them in esteem. Such a situation is a phenomenon worthy of a marketing study when it is considered that the CPA is restrained by ethical considerations from advertising.

In contrast, service bureaus do not usually enjoy the same privileged position in a client's confidence. Many business firms, especially smaller firms, will not consider dealing with a service bureau without the express approval of their CPA. Frequently, the CPA has a very limited knowledge of service bureaus, yet his opinion will often decide the fate of their proposals. Recognizing this situation, many service bureaus actively seek working relationships with CPA firms. In an address before ADAPSO, an executive of the industry made the following comments:

Make a point of finding out who the CPA or accountant is for each of your customers. Arrange to meet the accountant and let him get to know you and your service. Oftentimes an accounting firm will specialize in a certain type of client, such as hospitals, or construction firms, or whatever. Each client of his in the same field as your mutual client should become a potential customer. Ask him for references to these clients. Again, I say, sell the accountant and the customer is half sold. Many businesses will look to their accountants for advice in this area.[1]

During the first ADAPSO Management Symposium, a service bureau president stated that with respect to prospective customers, "where the accountants recommend us we have no problem at all."[2]

Each of the service bureaus interviewed during the field research phase of this study was quite cognizant of the privileged position CPAs enjoyed with their clients. However, the interviewees felt that the CPAs' privileged position was frequently detrimental to clients. Many convincing examples were cited amply illustrating many CPAs' general lack of appreciation for the capabilities of electronic data processing. The examples primarily pertained to small local CPA firms serving relatively small business firms, the kind many service bureaus actively solicit.

The literature search and interviews with CPAs and service bureaus permit the following generalization: service bureaus have been an aid to countless business firms. In addition, the profession stands to benefit from cooperation with service bureaus. Many service bureaus are willing to assist practitioners, formally and informally, who wish to learn about electronic data processing. Simultaneously, practitioners can prepare themselves to serve as important links in improved management information systems. Unfortunately, the majority of CPAs seem not to be aware of such benefits. A national CPA firm's former data processing consultant enunciated the problem succinctly when he commented, "CPA firms in the United States have their heads in the sand—and they won't pull their heads out, to see their opportunity in time to effectively participate in the service bureau industry."[3]

It should be noted that competent professionals in every field consult with one another on a regularly recurring basis in order to perform a given task more proficiently. The implication is evident. A professional in every class of work is committed to achieving a high degree of excellence in that field. To do so implies the utilization of the latest pertinent developments. All of these developments and their methods of application cannot be known entirely to one person or group. Consultation is the professional solution. In the field of information technology, when a competent service bureau and a progressive CPA consult with one another, they assure themselves that common clients will receive the finest management information systems possible. Ethical considerations which appear to preclude such an arrangement should be subject to question.

Assuming that the accounting profession recognizes the potential of service bureaus, a part of the distance to an effective working relationship between CPAs, their clients, and service bureaus is quickly covered. The ideal relationship evolves when the CPA performs effectively the role of catalyst. Such a role is not difficult to play, given the general attitude of clients toward CPAs and the desire of the majority of service bureaus to cooperate with CPAs. The key then is the accounting profession's recognition of the capabilities of service bureaus.

CATEGORIES OF SERVICE BUREAU EMPLOYMENT

The CPA finds that there are four general categories of service bureau use available for his clients:
1. Automation of financial statements and general ledger
2. Automation of clerical functions
3. Automation of decision making and control
4. Automation of the management information system

Each succeeding category contains the elements of each preceding category, so that the fourth category is the most comprehensive and the most sophisticated in its results. In addition, every category reflects a stage in a particular client's growth, in that changes in the size and complexity of his operations require a change in the category of service bureau employment. Each succeeding category assumes a greater need for information on the part of the client and greater degrees of expertise from the CPA and service bureau.

Prior to examining each of these categories, it may be useful to examine several general considerations the CPA faces when a service bureau is employed to serve clients.

General Considerations

The addition of the service bureau to the CPA-client team requires that the CPA examine the following considerations:

1. The desirability of package programs
2. The CPA's place in the flow of data
3. The form of transmitted data
4. The preparer of machine-sensible data
5. The method of transporting data

These considerations are separated for purposes of analysis only. In practice, their interaction requires them to be considered jointly.

The desirability of package programs. Package programs are commonly marketed by service bureaus to a variety of organizations. To the CPA considering service bureau applications for his clients, the cost characteristics of package programs are important. Indeed, for smaller clients, these are frequently the sole determinant. On the other hand, his clients' existing systems may not be compatible with available package programs, even though a variety of such programs is frequently available for many types of applications. In order to realize the cost benefits inherent in package programs, users must often adhere to the rather rigid specifications of a particular application. Generally, this necessitates some systems changes, many of them relatively minor. CPAs and their clients are often critical of this inflexibility. However, field research uncovered a number of examples where imaginative practitioners had effectively overcome restrictions peculiar to the package programs with which they were involved.[4] This was especially true where smaller clients were concerned. In addition, several practitioners noted that the preparation for a service bureau application was fruitful in terms of refining clients' existing systems and procedures.

At some point, package program applications are not feasible. This is certainly true as clients' information needs approach the fourth of the four categories of service bureau employment cited earlier. By that time, the increased benefits of custom-designed programs may far outweigh their greater costs.

The CPA's place in the flow of data. This is another important consideration in service bureau applications. There are two basic approaches. In some situations, the CPA collects data from a client, sends them to the service bureau, and receives the finished information directly from the service bureau. This arrangement places the CPA in a position of control and allows him to examine a client's data to ascertain their accuracy and clarity, and to eliminate unnecessary communication and processing problems for the service bureau. In addition, an examination of a client's newly processed information permits timely recommendations and allows the CPA to devise his own checking procedures for strengthening the reliability of the processed information. The approach described is common where smaller clients receive bookkeeping assistance from a CPA.

When clients send the data to the service bureau and receive the processed information from it, the CPA loses some measure of control, since he is not acting as an intermediary. Such a situation is rectified by checking the controls in the service bureaus' and the clients' systems. Such checks may require a test of the service bureaus' error correction procedures for inaccurate data received from customers, for machine failure, or for failure to use the correct customers' permanent records while processing weekly transactions. (The latter type of error may be practically impossible if certain checks are built into the applicable programs.) Clients' procedures for controlling the data flow to the service bureaus and for verifying the accuracy of processed records may be tested. Generally, the situation described is characteristic of clients receiving clerical or decision-making and control assistance in such matters as payroll and job scheduling.

The form of transmitted data. Another important consideration, closely allied to the previous one, is the form in which data are sent to the service bureau. The alternative data forms available are source documents, microfilms, adding machine tapes, listings of transactions, punched paper tapes, punched cards, and electrical impulses. Each form has characteristics with implications relating to the equipment needed for preparing data in a particular form, the cost and ease of transporting data to and from the service bureau, and data confidentiality, control, and security. Trade-offs between characteristics are common. For example, if source documents are sent to the service bureau, transportation costs may be excessive, and data confidentiality, control and security are minimal. In addition, while most costs associated with electronic data processing have been decreasing, the cost of preparing punched cards from source documents has not. However, special items of equipment or operators are unnecessary. The service bureau provides both. Alternatively, data transmitted in the form of punched paper tape is transported cheaply, and data confidentiality, control and security are greatly enhanced. For one thing, the punched tape can be lost without catastrophic consequences. In addition, tape-to-card converters are standard equipment in most service bureaus. This alternative eliminates the service bureau's personnel from the role of preparing data in machine-sensible form and correspondingly strengthens control. However, equipment and operator requirements shift from the service bureau to either the CPA or his clients.

The preparer of machine sensible data. A concomitant consideration is to determine who will prepare the data in machine-sensible form and send them to the service bureau. Here the implications are similar to those relating to the form of the transmitted data. For maximum data confidentiality, control and security, and for minimum transportation problems, the client and the CPA, in that order, should prepare the data. However, an investment by the client or the CPA in some type of input device may be necessary.

Methods of data preparation which require some type of input device, as opposed to completely manual methods, are widely employed by CPAs and their clients. Time saving is an important factor. The simplest such device is the ordinary adding machine. By using the non-add key to print numbers that identify the client, the journal, and the accountant, and by depressing the subtraction key for credits, the tape provides the necessary information for service bureau personnel to prepare machine-sensible input. During the past few years, adding machines equipped with an optical type font (numerals which can be read by some items of electronic equipment) have been successfully developed and marketed. However, a more publicized approach for source document preparation is the add-punch, a perforated paper tape-producing machine. The add-punch is often electrically connected to an adding machine or it can appear as a single item of equipment, a punched tape-adding machine. An advantage of the last two devices is the elimination of service bureau personnel in the preparation of input data.

Additional considerations which are germane for the client and CPA, assuming one of them prepares the data into machine-sensible form, are the availability of personnel and the effect of a specialized device (such as an add-punch) on the office routine. Small clients may not be able to justify devices beyond an adding machine and they may not have personnel capable of performing data preparation tasks. If the CPA acts as data preparer, he has similar considerations. In addition, add-punch machines are rather noisy and thus may disrupt the office routine. Office space considerations may also arise.

The method of transporting data. Data may be transported to and from the service bureau by a variety of methods. Postal services and messengers are the most common. Of course, each method has its own peculiar cost and security implications. During the past few years, there have been some interesting developments in the use of commercial telephone lines as a method of transmission. For example, in 1965 Monroe Data Processing installed a data-transmission device in an accountant's office in Alexandria, Virginia.[5] Data taken directly from clients' records are transmitted to a service bureau in Orange, New Jersey, by means of a punched tape-adding machine attached to a Dataphone. At the service bureau, the data are compiled and processed into various reports and analyses. Currently, these are mailed to the CPA. In the future, it is expected that the completed information will be transmitted back to the CPA via Dataphone. Similar data-transmission devices are being used for billing and payroll operations, the data being transmitted by the client from his place of business.[6]

It is submitted that such developments demand that the CPA venture into areas previously not considered to be within the bounds of accounting. From an audit standpoint, it appears that the CPA must comment on the reliability of the various methods of data transmission employed by his clients. The problem, then, is how does an auditor test a communications system? These are integral parts of information systems and they will be even more important in the near future.

The Automation of the Financial Statements and General Ledger

The first of the four general categories of service bureau employment available for serving clients is the automation of the financial statements and a general ledger. This is a very common service bureau application for relatively small clients. Generally, such an application is processed with a package program. These are two approaches.

Write-up work. The earliest accounting literature referring to service bureaus extolled their merits as an escape from the drudgery associated with write-up work, a high-volume, low-profit service many CPAs perform for clients too small to employ a bookkeeper. It usually follows this manual routine: monthly, the accountant obtains the client's source documents and then proceeds to make entries in the journals and postings to the ledger. At this point, he prepares the unadjusted trial balance, the necessary adjusting and closing entries, and the post-closing trial balance. By the time the financial statements are completed, the accountant often finds himself without time for profitably rendering additional services to the client, assuming the general case in which write-up services are performed for a fixed nominal fee. Often, the results are a client who cannot fully appreciate the potential managerial information in financial statements and an accountant who does not experience a feeling of professional accomplishment with each completed engagement.

In the late 1950's, service bureaus began having limited success with marketing package programs for general ledger and financial statement preparation. Many CPAs recognized the potential of this situation and began servicing write-up clients through service bureaus. Today, the same service is available, very often through service bureaus employing the latest electronic computers and featuring improved and expanded package programs.

For each client, CPAs must often choose from among several package programs, and from within a selected program they must decide which options to select. For example, general packages compatible with the requirements of firms in several industries are available as well as specialized package programs resigned exclusively for a particular industry. Within a program, various options provide services beyond the preparation of simple financial statements and the general ledger. For instance, percentages, year-to-date figures, comparative statements, and various subsidiary ledgers are available. Of course, the extras often are more expensive. As in selecting the program, the CPA will select those options whose values exceed their cost. One of the costs considered is the necessity of modifying a satisfactory system in order to be able to use a package program.

Periodic noncertified reports. The practice of preparing periodic financial statements for smaller clients employing at least a one-man bookkeeping staff, without rendering an opinion as to fairness of such statements, is often referred to as a non-opinion audit. In more formal terms, this practice is termed a periodic, usually monthly, noncertified report. The typical client receiving this service is larger than the typical write-up client. Non-opinion audits have been described by a practicing CPA thus:

Our practice is made up predominantly of monthly noncertified reports, where the client's personnel have written up the books of original entry, and our function, aside from our normal accounting procedures, verification, and tying in of various control accounts, consisted of the following semi-skilled functions:
1. Posting books of original entry to a general ledger
2. Taking off a trial balance
3. Preparing pencil copy of balance sheet and profit and loss statement monthly (with occasional percentage analysis)
4. Typing balance sheet and profit and loss statement monthly.[7]

The approach taken by this practitioner's firm for employing a service bureau is to continue to perform the usual accounting procedures, verifications, etc., but to eliminate the necessity of doing any of the four semiskilled functions outlined above. The procedure, which varies with client, industry, complexity, internal control, etc., employs "pick-off sheets" to recapitulate books of original entry and "tie-in sheets" to reconcile various details to controls. As emphasized by the firm, the basic difference between the procedures employed for servicing write-up clients and for preparing noncertified reports is that the client journalizes the books of original entry and posts to the general ledger.

There are a number of advantages to this approach, economic and professional. In the first place, because the client maintains his own journals, thus summarizing his accounting transactions, the service bureau's processing fee is less than in situations where each transaction is handled separately. There are fewer line items to record because the column total of a journal is treated as one line item. However, this saving is often more apparent than real. The cost of manually preparing the journals may more than offset the higher processing fee. Secondly, the time taken in the CPA's office to transform source data into machine-sensible form is reduced as opposed to performing write-up work. The practitioner referred to earlier estimated a ten-minute preparation time per client.[8] Finally, this approach allows the CPA time for performing other services for his clients.

A disadvantage of this approach is that added steps must be undertaken if machine analyses of sales, purchases, etc., are desired.

Such steps are unnecessary if financial statement preparation is the only service-bureau output desired. Clients receiving noncertified reports often find that financial statements are adequate managerial information. Furthermore, the cost of various analyses may exceed their value. For instance when financial statements need to be supplemented with various analyses, but the service-bureau processing costs are prohibitive, manual devices such as key-sort cards and pegboards may be feasible alternatives.

The Automation of Clerical Functions

The automation of clerical functions is particularly important in periods when skilled employees are in short supply. Rather than permit proficient office personnel to perform such time-consuming functions as payroll preparation, customer billing and the preparation of ancillary records, service bureaus may advantageously fill the need. First, office personnel can be used to perform a higher level of work, often increasing their satisfaction and the office's productivity. Secondly, service bureau applications of this type provide a wealth of analytical information in addition to the basic documents and records. For example, payroll processing can produce the checks, the check register, separate employee earning records, tax information, labor distribution, and analyses of labor costs. Similarly from a processing run of receivables the logical next step is the preparation of customer statements and various sales analyses. Prepared manually, these documents and records consume a great amount of time which could be put to more productive uses.

Most firms using a service bureau without going through their CPA generally obtain clerical processing assistance. Applications of this type appear to benefit only those firms whose clerical work volume is large enough to justify their own bookkeeping or accounting staffs. But this is not always the case. One service bureau interviewee told of a CPA who grouped the payrolls of a number of relatively small clients, prepared the data into machine-sensible form, and had the payroll processed by a service bureau. By grouping several firms' records and processing them as one, he was able to justify the cost of processing.

At the most sophisticated end of this category, several service bureau package systems, as opposed to programs, are available. Package systems, a group of related programs capable of processing financial statements, general ledger, and various clerical requirements, are available in conjunction with small-scale equipment.[9] One such complete system, the Burroughs Basic Record Control System, combines journal posting and document preparation by the client on a Burroughs posting machine, with financial statements, general ledger, and analytical reports processing by the service bureau. The machine produces a by-product punched paper tape which is the input to the service bureau.

The Automation of Decision-Making and Control Functions

At some point, a client reaches the stage where operations contain so many variables that it becomes difficult to make even basic decisions. For example, as a firm's inventory grows in absolute size, in turnover, and in the number of different line items, inventory control becomes correspondingly critical. Reorder points, recorder quantities, lead times, holding costs, ordering costs and other critical variables pertaining to inventory decisions are difficult to organize and control. Similar problems exist in production scheduling, procurement, freight routing, etc.

For this category of service bureau employment, a number of package programs are available. For example, the Service Bureau Corporation has a package program for automobile dealers' parts departments. The program automatically prepares purchase orders based on the consideration of such factors as economic order quantity and optimal reorder point, which in turn are derived from a consideration of lead time, holding and order costs, stock out costs, and a factor for parts turnover. The program also prepares an exception report which highlights slow moving items. Similarly, there are package PERT programs useful to contractors or firms involved in complex projects with many interrelated, although organizationally separate, functions. In addition, linear programming, simulation, market analysis, and transportation analysis package programs are available to aid decision making and control; more are being planned for scientific, mathematical, technical, and operations research applications.[10]

This particular category of service bureau employment demands a high level of expertise on the part of the CPA providing management services for his clients. It is important that the CPA recognize situations where such applications can be used. Furthermore, he should assist the client in selecting a suitable package program or aid him in preparing meaningful specifications for a custom-designed program. Such programs are quite common in this category of service bureau employment especially when it is desirable to effectively integrate already interdependent areas such as procurement, production and inventory.

An additional observation is in order. A management interested first in the high-speed solution to decision-making problems is confronted with an interesting paradox: it will probably enjoy the greatest long-term benefits a computer can offer, but it will probably be among the last to have a machine of its own.[11] Because such applications are difficult to program yet typically require few machine hours to solve, a computer may be underutilized. "To those who give priority to programming the decision-making problems first, the service bureau is a natural ally."[12]

The Computerization of the
Management Information System

The final category of service bureau employment is not nearly as important today as it will be within the next few years, with forthcoming innovations in communications equipment, computers, peripheral equipment, and software. In Chapter VI the implications of these developments are examined in greater detail.

As a firm's operation size and complexity increase, but by current standards not enough for an on-premises computer installation, the complete automation of integrated financial records, clerical functions, decision models, control techniques, etc., often becomes desirable. At the present time, very little, if anything, is being done through service bureaus in establishing a completely computerized management information system of the type described in Chapter II. Communications equipment and software, among others, present limitations. However, partially-computerized management information systems through a service bureau exist, given custom-designed programs and available communications equipment.

It is submitted that this category of service bureau employment is the one to which the public accounting profession must address itself. This, too, is an area where the challenge of information technology will be quite evident. The implications for management services and auditing engagements are staggering. Within the next few years, demands which can only be successfully met by information technologists will be made upon the profession. The rewards and penalties are great. One way for the individual practitioner to prepare himself for a share of the rewards is through the experience gained from service bureau applications, especially the more sophisticated ones.

SELECTING A SERVICE BUREAU

CPAs are traditionally careful about embarking upon new ventures which may substantially modify their methods of operation. While the reasons cited for this attitude are often couched in theoretical or ethical terms, it is submitted that pragmatic factors should receive their share of consideration. Adherence to tried and tested practices, I am convinced, retains clients, whereas the unfavorable outcome of an innovative practice may have undesireable repercussions.

An attitude of care with respect to new undertakings is admirable if it does not undermine progress. With respect to selecting a service bureau, an attitude of care is essential because of the disparity in their levels of competence. Selection begins with an identification of problem areas in a system which could be aided by a service bureau application. Then, an analysis of alternative aids is in order. Finally, assuming that a service bureau application is chosen, selection criteria should be developed to aid in selecting a competent organization.

Situations For Service Bureau Applications

Situations in which a client could use a service bureau fall into several categories. A functional method of differentiation based on use is selected to describe certain categories which supplement the four levels of service bureau use discussed earlier.

Branch office processing. The continued advances in communications allow service bureaus to be linked together by data transmission networks thus enabling them to transfer data and to use each other's facilities.[13] For clients with distant divisions, sales offices, plants, and warehouses, a service bureau located near such installations processes the data applicable to overall company operations and then transmits them to the central service bureau, which compiles the data into management reports, records, etc. Service bureaus at the distant installations process such items as the local payroll or provide assistance in setting up the shop schedule for the following day. The latter application may be affected by considerations transmitted from the home office via the central service bureau. In effect, such a system is comparable to a company-owned central processor maintaining communications with its branch operations.

One-time or occasional applications. Often, clients with their own data processing installations have specialized commercial or scientific problems which require special equipment, specially-trained personnel, and very sophisticated programs. For example, many scientific problems are better suited for analog computers rather than digital computers. A systems-design problem which may require the modification of an existing system may be better handled by a service bureau's systems analyst. In addition, service bureaus have libraries of special programs which would be prohibitive in cost for most firms.

Peak-load elimination. Many clients with their own automated data-processing installations find it expedient and economical to use a service bureau for eliminating regularly recurring peak working demands. The limitations of an installation's capacity may be especially evident at period-end or at payroll-preparation time. The majority of these limitations are clerically oriented, placing great demands on the input and output capabilities of a system. In the case of a computerized system, such a condition represents a significant under-utilization of the computer's computational capabilities. Rather than accept late exception reports, shop loading plans, etc., because of payroll, billing or some other clerical requirements, many companies send the "dirty work" to a service bureau.

Unexpected overloads. Clients with their own installation can be directed to service bureaus for aid in the elimination of temporary overload conditions caused by equipment failure and employee absenteeism or turnover. In addition, special requirements such as mailing advertising material, preparing a special price catalogue, etc., may disrupt routine. Again, the service bureau can be called upon to render assistance. An important advantage of this kind of application is that costly overtime hours are kept to a minimum.

Clients installing computers. Clients installing their own computers or tabulating equipment can receive assistance from a service bureau. The operation of equipment configurations similar to those being considered for installation can be observed and evaluated and trial runs of clients' data can be processed. When the equipment has been selected, the CPA may suggest that the client's personnel undergo a training period at the service bureau while the equipment is on order. The service bureau may also provide personnel to assist in designing the new system. In addition, when the equipment arrives, the service bureau can be used as a parallel operation until such time as the client's installation has passed certain tests.

The Selection Process

Detailed procedural lists often mislead rather than enlighten if their purpose is misconstrued.[14] Being general in nature, check lists should be modified to reflect the conditions associated with a specific purpose. This section lists and describes some of the basic considerations in selecting a service bureau.

Problem definition. Prior to contacting a service bureau, the problem area and its specifications should be defined as explicitly as possible. The CPA has a very important contribution to make because of his intimate knowledge of a client's existing system and future requirements. A part of his contribution will be to supply detailed answers to such questions as the following:

1. Which type of information or data processing is required?
2. What will be the disposition of such information or data processing?
3. Which is the desired form of the data to be sent to the service bureau?
4. Which is the desired form of the work received from the service bureau?
5. How frequently must the information or processing be available?
6. Will a period of parallel operations be necessary?

Without exception, defining the problem is the most important step in the entire selection process. Too often, a client approaches the service bureau without a clear statement of the problem. The service bureau finds itself in the awkward position of attempting to provide a service without having adequate guidelines. The result often is an application costing more than it should while concurrently providing few benefits. Thus, service bureaus gain a critic, and the client and the CPA lapse into an unreasonable mistrust of electronic data processing.

A well planned problem definition will almost always result in a successful application. From such a definition, a competent and reputable service bureau can decide whether or not an application can be undertaken which will meet a client's expectations. In addition to the problem definition, the service bureau should be provided with a description of the client's existing system and underlying procedures as an aid in understanding the problem definition.

Requirements placed on the service bureau. A step related to that of problem definition is the determination of the requirements placed on the service bureau in terms of its performance, responsibility, and integration into a client's system. If the service bureau application is for management decision making and control, this step is especially critical; however, for most clerical applications, the requirements placed upon a service bureau are relatively minor.

For the former type of application, the service bureau becomes an integral part of a client's management information system. It operates, with respect to the client, in a manner similar to that of a large corporation's central processor serving many remote divisions or departments. Under such circumstances, the service bureau is expected to make certain commitments for delivering information on a timely basis, processing a reasonable amount of special requirements, assuring a suitable degree of accuracy, and guaranteeing the confidentiality of a client's records. In addition, adequate controls over processing and over a client's records maintained by the service bureau are essential. Of course, there are other requirements which will vary from application to application. These must be determined in advance of the actual engagement.

For financial records and clerical applications, many of the same requirements exist. However, the relative degree of importance will not be the same. For example, timeliness may be important, though not critical. On the other hand, the requirement for confidentiality will not differ.

Obtain competitive bids. The names of local service bureaus can be secured from the classified directory of the telephone book, and from other CPAs dealing with service bureaus. In addition, ADAPSO publishes an annual directory of members. Several trade periodicals publish annual issues containing the names and locations of various service bureaus. One even gives a description of the services offered by firms responding to its questionnaire. The best sources of referral are often CPAs with service bureau experience. The point is that service bureaus are different in terms of personnel, equipment, specialties, competence, dependability, reputability, and, of course, price.

Form a selection committee. A selection committee, composed of a representative from each of the functional areas to be affected by the service bureau application, other interested parties within the firm, and the CPA, should investigate a number of service bureaus, then select certain ones to submit proposals based on the problem definition. During the investigation phase, the committee should find answers to the following questions:

1. How successful has the service bureau been with similar proposals in the past?
2. How well capitalized is the organization? Will financial difficulty preclude it from processing the client's needs in the foreseeable future?
3. If future changes in the client's requirements were made, could the service bureau accommodate them?
4. Is the service bureau noted for being aware of new developments in its field and incorporating them where applicable?
5. What kind of a reputation for cooperation does it have?
6. Does it employ an effective system of controls which will satisfy an auditor?

Evaluate the service bureau proposals. At this point, the service bureau proposals requested should be subjected to a careful analysis, operational as well as financial. Such factors as each proposal's technical competence, completeness, price, etc., should be carefully reviewed. Again, it must be emphasized that the quality of a service bureau's proposal is dependent upon the problem definition submitted by the client.

The service bureau's completed proposal should be quite comprehensive. For decision-making and control applications, it may contain suggestions for the modification of input media, completed reports, and the client's existing system and procedures. Suggestions for additional information or the deletion of certain reports or parts thereof may be made. The proposal may go so far as to recommend the acquisition of equipment, such as a bookkeeping machine or Dataphone communications, in order to make the service bureau and client more compatible. In addition to the modifications mentioned, the service bureau's proposal should delineate its responsibility to the client. This would include the following, some of which were considered earlier:

1. To study future requirements when requested by the customer and to make recommendations.
2. To design, develop, and thoroughly test the best possible system, given its cost, and to handle the customer's processing.
3. To arrange and maintain a realistic delivery schedule.
4. To set up every necessary control to insure the accuracy of the customer's reports.
5. To guarantee that all the customer's work will be handled in the strictest confidence.
6. To guarantee against the loss or damage of the customer's documents.[15]

A detailed cost breakdown, with limits stated where uncertainty exists, should be included. The service bureau should present a statement, again for guidance on control applications, which states specific goals for the completion of the job. A measure of control can be exercised over the production schedule by comparing the statement against future invoices for services rendered as of a certain date.

The proposal for financial record or clerical applications is often similar in general content but shorter and less detailed than a proposal for a control application. Its main concern will be the delivery schedule, the controls of processing, and the confidentiality of data. Because proposals of this type are often quite similar between service bureaus, the main selection criterion will probably be price, assuming that the competence and reputation of each submitter are equal.

An important financial consideration to remember when evaluating service bureaus' proposals is that they include almost all costs. By comparison, the costs of alternatives to using a service bureau, including the existing system, often exclude certain less obvious costs. The costs of personnel, supplies, maintenance, space, repairs, air-conditioning units, electricity, heat, insurance, taxes, etc., should be added to an equipment manufacturer's equipment rental charges in order that that alternative may be comparable to the expense of using a service bureau.[16] However, certain costs should also be added to a service bureau's proposal. On the objective side, the cost of messenger services or of a communications link to the service bureau must be considered. Similar treatment should be accorded subjective costs such as the late delivery of information or the possible loss of documents, at least to the extent that such costs exceed the similar costs of other alternatives.

Additional Considerations

Concurrent with the selection of a service bureau, the CPA should examine several related considerations. Among these are the types of contracts and methods of charging, processing controls, protection of clients' records, and provisions for a periodic systems review.

Types of contracts and methods of charging. There are three common types of contracts provided by service bureaus. These are fixed price, time and materials, and cost-plus-fixed-fee or percentage.[17] An important factor to remember is that because there are incompetent organizations in the service bureau industry just as in other industries, all contracts should provide a means for cancellation or withdrawal if the client is not satisfied. A good service bureau will be willing to do this.

The estimation of some service costs is an industry-wide problem. This fact should influence which type of contract the client selects for a given application. The cost of using a package program is usually easily estimated, while that of developing a custom-designed program or even a complete system is difficult to determine. For package applications, running time is easily estimated and program development costs are known. A standard rate charged is intended to recover the costs of development and processing and an increment of profit. In terms of custom-designed applications, programmers cannot be judged by efficiency standards used for the production line. In addition to the uncertainty shrouding its preparation, there is the difficult task of estimating a non-existent program's processing time.

The problem becomes more complex if the service bureau is undercapitalized, because it cannot accept losses on many jobs. Consequently, the tendency may be to underplay the complexity of a problem hoping that once the contract is signed, the necessary funds will come forth to complete the job.[18] One way that the CPA can protect the client is to ascertain that the problem definition contains few, if any, areas subject to more than one interpretation. In addition, the CPA should meet the people who will design the application and determine their standard job titles and salary rates.[19] This knowledge serves as a future safeguard against the adverse effects of personnel turnover. Above all, the CPA should require parallel documentation for clients' programs in the developmental stage to protect against such effects. In addition, the contract should unequivocally state the ownership of the program, specification sheets, card layouts, flow charts, and other underlying documentation.

In general, fixed price contracts are best suited for the relatively easy jobs which use package programs. For custom-designed applications, one of the other two contract types is usually superior. For example, if by chance one or both parties fail to recognize a real problem area, the quality of the project may suffer. Consequently, a time and materials or cost-plus-fixed-fee contract is best; it should cover such aspects as partial payments, acceptance, and final completion. The contract should also provide for future modifications to the original work.

In terms of rate structure, some service bureaus' charges include that for central processor and off-line equipment usage, the latter at no extra cost up to some reasonable amount. In other cases, there is a separate charge for both. The charge for supplies may also vary. Programming time is, of course, always extra, as may be the cost of an extensive systems proposal. Furthermore, there are often premium charges for priority, convenience, and first-shift processing.[20]

As for the range of charges, the Service Bureau Corporation reports that some customers pay as little as $15 per month, while others are charged as much as $20,000 per month.[21] Coleman and Cohn cite a number of cases where clients receive some combination of sophisticated management reports and clerical processing for charges of $165 to $375 per month.[22] MAP 18 describes the following billing rates, which apply to write-up type applications as of 1963:

1. Set up charges ranging from $5 to $25.
2. Fixed charges for each report period (varies according to the amount of machine time, labor and overhead).
3. Charges for each descriptive item requiring words to be printed on financial statements, including captions and account titles.
4. Charges for each balance carried forward in an account from the close of the previous period including balances of zero.
5. Charges varying from 1½ to 7 cents per transaction during the current period.
6. Miscellaneous charges for correcting errors, making changes in the chart of accounts, providing extra copies of ledgers and

statements, filing cards for subsequent reruns and supplemental statements, etc.[23]

One possible way to reduce rates is to have the client prepare the data in machine-sensible form, preferably as a by-product of the recorded event. While the service bureau's processing costs have declined with technological progress, the cost of key-punching has not.

Processing controls.[24] The CPA should be familiar with the error detection and control devices designed into a computer's circuitry and into the programs employed. This is an important audit consideration when rendering services to clients with their own computer installation. However, when a client's reports and records are completely or partially processed off the premises, additional steps are necessary to protect the auditor and the client. Where the computer is located at a service bureau, control over certain aspects of the processing are difficult. Examples of these are:

1. deviations by operators from the standard instructions
2. inclusion of extraneous input data
3. conditions not provided for in the instructions
4. errors in input data cards or tapes where prepared by the bureau
5. print-out errors.[25]

In addition, records sent to the service bureau or the client's files maintained by the service in the form of magnetic tapes, discs, or punched cards can be lost, misplaced, or altered.

It is the client's responsibility to ascertain that prior to initial processing, the files maintained by the service bureau are printed out and compared to the original records. The service bureau then should be responsible for maintaining strict control of these files. The nature of the control must be outlined to the CPA.

At the start of an application, there should always be a period of parallel operation long enough to assure that the new system is operating properly. In conjunction with the processing, the service bureau must supply the CPA a detailed narrative description or flowchart of the client's application as it moves through the service bureau. The flow chart or description should show the various control points in the processing system. This includes action from the receipt of the client's data to the receipt of the finished job by the client. Considered therein would be the procedures and controls employed in preparing a job for processing, to include key-punching and machine room preparation, processing either by the computer or peripheral equipment, and preparing the job in the form desired by the client. Each step of the way must evidence a standardized, orderly work flow with written procedures in force for ordinary as well as exception routines. Such a document should be a part of the client's permanent file maintained by the CPA. Any changes must have some pre-planned method of being reported to the CPA.

In addition to the programs used for processing his clients, the controls designed into these programs and the processing routine, the CPA must be concerned with the physical safeguarding of these programs. Programs are a part of the system; as such they must be examined and safeguarded regardless of the fact that the computer is not on the client's premises. In fact, this is all the more reason why the programs, the controls designed into them, and the physical control exercised over them should be examined. Standard procedures for writing programs should also be evident, especially if a client is having custom programs prepared.

These procedures should include standard methods of performing particular operations which would facilitate the reading of the programs for amendment and revision purposes at a later date and also for insertion of standard checks which may be considered, bearing in mind the design of the machine.[26]

Such documentation is essential but often nonexistent. Documentation permits a universal understanding of a programmer's work and allows another to complete the work if need be.

Although the CPA should maintain a copy of the programs used by his clients, service bureaus often hesitate to make package programs available to outsiders. In such instances, the CPA should recognize that package programs represent a large outlay by the service bureau. Such programs are similar to specialized fixed assets whose costs are partially recovered each time a sale is made. The service bureau must be convinced that the CPA will maintain the confidentiality of such programs. In the case of custom-designed programs, the ownership of the program usually is with the client. Changes to programs used by clients must be authorized by a designated person and the CPA should be given a copy of such changes.

The checks designed into programs used by clients are important to an auditor in his examination of a client's system. Ideally, a schedule of such checks and their location in the program should be compiled and made available to the CPA. Record counts, hash totals, proof figures, reverse multiplication, limit checks, cross-footing balance-checks, check points, self-checking numbers, sequence checks, and other such control measures enable him to carry out his job more effectively. While warnings are often given about the processing and programming time wasted by an auditor's overcontrol, the internal speeds of second and third generation computers are such as to lessen appreciably the importance of these warnings. Finally, all pertinent matters relative to processing controls should be clearly specified in the contract.

Protection of client records. The protection of client records has several aspects; among these are the protection from theft and destruction, the maintenance of their confidentiality, and the assurance of their accuracy. Physical protection from theft should be evidenced in the internal procedures of the service bureau. For example, entrance into the record storage and processing areas should be restricted. Programs should be maintained and controlled in a library. Records should receive a similar measure of control. Documents arriving for processing and which will be returned to a customer should be logged in and controlled throughout their stay in the service bureau.

Fire resistant cabinets and safes should be available for client's records and there should be a system for designating the degree of importance of records. Such a system would aid in determining the types of safe-keeping devices to use. For vital records which would be all but impossible to reproduce, duplicate copies could be maintained at another location. For other records, reproducible but at considerable cost or inconvenience, there are available cabinets which are tested at 2000° F. for four hours with an inside temperature not exceeding 350° F.[27] Fire is an even greater hazard because magnetic tape, an increasingly popular method of storing records, is combustible at 150° F. Here, too, the CPA must ascertain the degree of protection his client is afforded.

The confidentiality of data depends greatly on the type of personnel the service bureau employs. A reputation for violating confidentiality makes itself known. The service bureau can, to a certain extent, protect itself and the client through fidelity bonds. However, a better method is for the client's documents to arrive at the service bureau in machine-sensible form, preferably identified only by a customer number. Of course, the key to customer numbers must be controlled. Where required for utmost security, the client or the CPA can monitor the processing of data and its complete movement through the service bureau.[28] A further aid would be the speedy, controlled return of processed data to the customer. The longer finished reports remain at the service bureau, the greater the probability of something undesirable happening. Finally, the means of moving data between the customer and service bureau should be subject to adequate control. Again, such control should be specified in the contract.

The processing controls discussed earlier are an effective means of assuring accuracy. Inaccuracies due to machine failure or personnel error must be guarded against. A knowledge of the internal machine checks and their coordination with program checks aids in attaining a high degree of accuracy. Personnel training is important in this respect as are good supervision, adherence to standardized procedures, and operable error detection and correction routines.

It has been suggested that larger service bureaus employ a trained internal auditor for overall protection of records and for processing control.[29] Assigned to the quality control department or to the administrative department, he can be an effective aid in improving the system of internal control. The internal auditor can also inject the customers' points of view into a service bureau's operations.[30] Are job costs in line with their benefits? Is there a better and less expensive way to achieve the same benefits? Are the CPA's control requests unrealistic? Are there better ways to meet his requirements? These and many related questions can be answered with advantage to all concerned. Smaller service bureaus can obtain similar benefits by engaging, on an intermittent basis, the services of CPA firms active in data processing.

Clients' responsibilities. Clients owe the service bureaus they employ certain responsibilities, some of which have been mentioned. When unreproducible documents are sent to the service bureau, duplicates should be retained to guard against the loss or destruction of originals. Problem definition has been stressed, yet this is a responsibility that the majority of service bureau customers neglect. The period of parallel processing has also been mentioned. Here again, some customers may be so anxious to switch over to their new systems that they neglect this important precaution. Computer programs provide burdens in addition to those created by a new system. All possible exceptions are difficult to foresee and thus are not included in a problem definition. These inevitably arise during the transition period. "Debugging" such a system is a must, as anyone familiar with electronics will attest.

In computer terminology there is the phrase, "garbage in—garbage out," which applies to the data some clients send to service bureaus. Clients must establish controls even if it is only by such a simple technique as an adding machine tape of a group of documents' balances. In addition, clients must deliver their data in readable or processable form, accurately prepared, and at the designated time.

Provisions for review. Periodically, the CPA should assist his clients by reviewing their existing systems. At these times improvements to the systems can be considered. In addition, it is an excellent time for reviewing the service bureaus' performance, the desirability of the reports generated, and other related matters. The following kinds of questions should be raised for each client's application:

1. Is the service bureau meeting the client's deadlines?
2. How effective has the service bureau's error control proved?
3. Are extra charges being billed which were not in the original contract?
4. Is the client satisfied with the new reports and procedures?
5. Could the contract be renewed at a lower fee now that the job has been debugged?
6. Should service bureau use be expanded?

An Example of a Service Bureau Rating Schedule

A formal service bureau rating schedule, prepared by the Research Institute of America, is included as a selection guide (see Figure IV-1). Of special interest are the relative weights placed on various factors.[31] The importance of a service bureau's proposal is paramount. Cost is second in relative importance, signifying that service considerations should take precedence over cost. The service bureau's experience and certain communication considerations are next in importance. However, the relative importance assigned to control considerations may surprise an auditor. As emphasized earlier, schedules of check lists are only guides and are certainly not substitutes for judgment.

How to Rate a Data Processing Center

Below are nine factors to consider in selecting an EDP center. To decide which one of two or more firms is best for your needs, simply mark the appropriate box next to each factor. Then add the numbers next to the boxes you've checked and compare the totals. (The numbers give greater weight to the more important features, such as cost.) Other things being equal, high score wins.

FACTORS	FACILITY A			FACILITY B		
	OK	So-So	Weak	OK	So-So	Weak
1. Nature of the proposal—how well it suits your needs, improves over present methods.	12 ☐	6 ☐	0 ☐	12 ☐	6 ☐	0 ☐
2. Cost — hourly rate, over-all charge, or per transaction.	10 ☐	5 ☐	0 ☐	10 ☐	5 ☐	0 ☐
3. Reputation or recommendation.	6 ☐	3 ☐	0 ☐	6 ☐	3 ☐	0 ☐
4. The sales representative—(Does he know his business? Is he clear on costs, services, etc.?)	4 ☐	2 ☐	0 ☐	4 ☐	2 ☐	0 ☐
5. Experience of other users.	6 ☐	3 ☐	0 ☐	6 ☐	3 ☐	0 ☐
6. Past experience in your industry or with your problem.	8 ☐	4 ☐	0 ☐	8 ☐	4 ☐	0 ☐
7. Appearance of physical facilities—orderly, clean, etc., geared to do a job.	6 ☐	3 ☐	0 ☐	6 ☐	3 ☐	0 ☐
8. Geographic proximity, convenience of working with firm.	8 ☐	4 ☐	0 ☐	8 ☐	4 ☐	0 ☐
9. Security and control, degree of responsibility for protecting your records, etc.	6 ☐	3 ☐	0 ☐	6 ☐	3 ☐	0 ☐
	Total_____			Total_____		

FIGURE IV-1

Reprinted by permission of the Research Institute of America, Management Report, "How to Choose and Use an Outside EDP Center," Copyright 1963 by the Research Institute of America.

ADVANTAGES AND DISADVANTAGES OF SERVICE BUREAU EMPLOYMENT

There are a number of possible advantages and disadvantages inherent in the employment of a service bureau which may affect both the client and the CPA. Most of these have been mentioned. A few of each are noted in this section.

Advantages of Service Bureau Employment

The potential of service bureaus can be realized to varying degrees by clients. In addition to decision-making and control applications which can assist a client in locating a new plant, evaluating bids, forecasting sales, and selecting economical transportation routes, the following day-to-day advantages are reported:

1. Generally faster and more reliable reports.
2. Elimination of turnover and absentee problems along with the elimination of supervision, training and overtime costs, particularly among clerical personnel.
3. Peak workloads during report-preparing time can be assumed by the Service Center.
4. Use of the Service Center as a training ground by firms considering a computer installation.
5. Closer control over processing costs because the Service Center charges vary directly with usage.
6. Transfer of the risks of equipment obsolescence to the Service Center.
7. Availability of the Service Center as a stand-by for the firm's own computer installation.[32]

The biggest advantage is the availability of trained specialists. This advantage serves as the basis for any other positive claims the service bureau can make. The availability of trained specialists assures maximum machine utilization while "most private installations are getting a 40% to 60% week rather than the conventional 40 hours because of improper utilization of equipment. A good center gets two hours more than there are in a week."[33]

For the CPA, the following advantages have been noted:

1. The use of service agencies can relieve the staff of a CPA firm of many time-consuming calculations.
2. The use of an agency may enable the CPA's staff to present detailed information breakdowns of a client's data which are often far too laborious and costly to perform in the usual manner.
3. With the exception of possibly acquiring one small piece of equipment, there is usually little investment required other than the time it takes to learn the necessary operations.
4. If the service is found to be uneconomical, equipment rentals can be terminated and the previous client-handling procedures can be resumed. (Agencies frequently recommend that the original method of handling a client should be maintained in parallel with EDP system for a short time until initial skepticism and misunderstanding are overcome.)

5. As a rule, service agencies provide a CPA with an EDP capability at a relatively low cost as compared with what he might pay to develop the same capability himself.
6. They allow the CPA to become acquainted with data processing with a minimum commitment on his part. There is also no need for the CPA to invest in expensive equipment, to acquire and train personnel or to wait a long time before obtaining benefits.
7. Serving a CPA's client through an agency can lead to an expansion of the services provided by the CPA to his clients.[34]

Disadvantages of Service Bureau Employment

During the January, 1963, ADAPSO management symposium, the results were presented of a state CPA society's survey evaluating member experiences with service bureaus.[35] It is interesting to note that half of the experiences were unfavorable. The important reasons given were:

1. Lack of timeliness.
2. Misunderstanding among service bureau, client, and accountant.
3. Inflexibility inherent in data processing operations.
4. Insufficient knowledge of CPA and client regarding the technicalities in handling work.
5. Lack of planning, particularly where client deals directly with the Service Center.[36]

An interview with a partner of a small CPA firm that had installed its own data processing equipment revealed another disadvantage. The firm would not have set up its own installation had its experience with service bureaus been satisfactory. The major criticism centered around the general lack of accounting orientation of service bureaus. This was particularly evident in audit trails which were generally inadequate for year-end work. In addition, the controls designed into the processing system could not be relied upon from an auditor's point of view.

Another important disadvantage which must be noted is that the shortage of trained personnel, while directly affecting the service bureau industry, plays havoc with clients. There appears to be no immediate solution except that the CPA must train himself to a level where he can differentiate between quality work and rubbish.

In a recent survey by the AICPA, some additional disadvantages peculiar to the CPA were noted. Among these are the following:

1. Use of a service agency introduces a third party into the CPA's dealings with his client. This may have the following disadvantages:

    (a) In some cases clients of the CPA submit or receive data directly through the agency. This may run counter to what the accountant feels is a desirable relationship to maintain with his client.

    (b) Records are usually maintained by the service agency which represent a cumulative history of a client's data. These are used to prepare comparative financial statements, to perform tax analyses, or any of several other management services. Unless duplicate records are maintained by the CPA, he must rely on the agency for proper maintenance and protection of this valuable data.

    (c) The fact that a client's data is in the hands of a third party may be considered a violation of the CPA's code of ethics.

    (d) Unless checks are made on the completeness and accuracy of the outputs produced by the agencies, the CPA may not have the personal assurance he gets when the work is done in his own office by his staff.

2. Computers do make mistakes, and when they do, it may be difficult to detect and correct them unless adequate checks and procedures are established to cope with them. For this reason, the CPA must perform his own checks on the data he submits and gets back from an agency. Furthermore, he should scrutinize, understand, and evaluate the internal checks of the agency, since much of their "automated" processing involves manual data preparation not unlike that of a CPA's own operations.

3. An additional cost is incurred by the CPA in order to deal with a service agency. In the case of relatively simple preprogrammed functions, the agency charges can be accurately estimated. However, for custom-designed programs, the cost of development and operation of a special computer application may be underestimated at the start and increase unexpectedly. Programmers very often underestimate the time it takes to write and test a program.

4. Another factor in relation to cost is that the price an agency places on the development of the exact program specified by the CPA may be uneconomical. The CPA then has to choose between a different (perhaps noncomputerized) solution to the problem or to compromise some of the requirements in order to simplify (and thus reduce the cost of) the desired computer program.[37]

V

The Effects of Data-Processing Service Bureaus on the Practice of Public Accounting in Michigan

The potential benefits from service bureau relationships for CPAs were examined in the preceding chapter. As it is based primarily upon a review of the literature and interviews with CPAs and service bureaus working together successfully, Chapter IV may represent a biased viewpoint. Successful service bureau applications create enthusiasm and inspire articles; average or poor experiences elicit relatively little interest and publicity. For that reason, surveys based on mailed questionnaires were undertaken to evaluate the extent of service bureau use and the service bureau relationships of a sample of Michigan CPA firms. In effect, the following hypotheses were being tested:

1. Differences exist between CPA firms involved and those not involved with service bureaus.
2. Differences exist between categories of CPA firms involved in various ways with service bureaus.

The differences may be in staff composition, client characteristics, attitudes, services rendered, and other such factors.

In this chapter, I examine the population sampled, the evaluation of the responses to each survey, and the conclusions drawn from the questionnaires.

The Population Sampled

The study consists of two surveys based upon the responses to three separate questionnaires. The major group surveyed was the member firms of the Michigan Association of Certified Public Accountants (MACPA). As of February, 1966, the MACPA membership lists of resident managing partners and sole practitioners numbered 564, representing approximately 87 percent of all CPA firms practicing in Michigan.[1] The other groups surveyed jointly were 64 service bureaus and 50 commercial banks located in Michigan. The service bureaus surveyed were selected from the 1965 telephone directory Yellow Pages of all Michigan cities with more than 10,000 inhabitants during the 1960 census. The 50 largest Michigan banks, in terms of financial resources, were selected from the February, 1966, *Michigan Manufacturer and Financial Record.*[2]

CPA Post Card Questionnaire

A two-part post card was sent to all member firms of the MACPA in February of 1966 (see Appendix A). Preprinted on the return portion of each post card were four descriptive categories and the name and address of a firm's resident managing partner or that of a sole practitioner.

The purpose of this post card questionnaire was to determine the nature of each firm's relationship with service bureaus and hence the extent of service bureau use by Michigan CPAs. By checking one or a combination of the four descriptive categories,, 448 respondents, approximately 80 percent of the MACPA's member firms, identified themselves and provided the solicited information.

The results of the post card questionnaire appear in Table V-1.[3]

Several noteworthy considerations appear in Table V-1. Foremost is the large number and proportion of CPA firms without any type of service bureau relationship. Even though the statistics may obscure factors influencing service bureau use, the number and proportion of non-users seem too great for the computer age. Implications such as the following may be valid:

1. CPA firms generally do not adequately understand automation or properly weigh its value as opposed to its cost.
2. Clients of many CPAs are at a competitive disadvantage by being denied benefits obtainable from service bureaus.

TABLE V-1

SERVICE BUREAU RELATIONSHIPS OF A
SAMPLE OF MICHIGAN CPA FIRMS

Category	Responding Firms Number	Responding Firms Percent
I — Firms not involved with service bureaus	252	56.2%
II — Firms with clients directly using service bureaus	120	26.8
III — Firms using outside service bureaus to service clients	38	8.5
IV — Firms in both Categories II and III	27	6.0
V — Firms with their own service bureaus	11	2.5
Total	448	100.0%

3. Professional associations face a tremendous task of upgrading their members' understanding of automation.

A second consideration relates to the number of CPA firms using service bureaus to serve clients as opposed to the number of CPA firms with clients directly using service bureaus. There are three times as many in the latter category as in the former. However, it seems this relationship should be reversed. It appears that small businesses without accounting staffs or with very small ones comprise the largest proportion of the total number of businesses. Further, it is reasonable to assume that many of these businesses obtain book-keeping assistance from CPA firms and that the majority of CPA firms service clients of this type. Consequently, if CPA firms providing such services do in fact recognize the benefits of automation, it would be expected that a greater number of them would use service bureaus to process the bookkeeping services they render. Therefore, it may be that:

1. CPA firms are performing a disproportionate amount of routine manual work.

2. The publicity devoted to the success of some CPA firms in automating write-up work has had a limited effect upon the profession as a whole.

A third consideration is that eleven of the responding firms use their own service bureau or one in which their firm has a financial interest. (Three additional CPA firms reported they would acquire computers during 1966.) These firms stand in sharp contrast to the firms described earlier. Although the ethical implications of service bureau ownership by a CPA firm are substantially unresolved (and are in any event beyond the scope of this study), equipment ownership *may* represent a positive approach to rendering improved services for clients and to providing staff training in electronic data processing.

I should emphasize that any inferences drawn are subject to qualifications: numerous underlying factors not explicitly identified undoubtedly affect Table V-1. In general, it appears that wide divergence exists in the practices employed by Michigan CPA firms to meet the challenges posed by information technology and that a disproportionate number may be relatively uninformed of the benefits from automation.

CPA Detailed Multi-Part Questionnaire

A detailed multi-part questionnaire mailed in April of 1966 served as the second phase of the CPA survey (see Appendix B). The 448 respondents to the post card questionnaire were sent the part or parts of the detailed questionnaire appropriate to their reported service bureau relationships. Firms which indicated that they operate their own service bureaus were considered a separate category regardless of any other service bureau relationship. A total of 123 firms responded, representing 27.5 percent of the post card questionnaire respondents or 21.8 percent of the MACPA's member firms (see Table V-2).[4] The following analyses of the responses to the detailed multi-part questionnaire test the hypotheses previously stated.

TABLE V-2
RESPONSE DISTRIBUTION TO THE SECOND
PHASE OF THE CPA SURVEY

Category	Responding Firms Number	Percent
I — Firms not involved with service bureaus	62	50.4%
II — Firms with clients directly using service bureaus	27	22.0
III — Firms using outside service bureaus to service clients	10	8.1
IV — Firms in both Categories II and III	16	13.0
V — Firms with their own service bureaus	8	6.5
Total	123	100.0%

*Differences Between CPA Firms Involved
and Not Involved with Service Bureaus*

The hypothesis that there are differences between CPA firms involved and those not involved with service bureaus appears valid.

The differences are examined below. Where necessary, statistical measures supporting the hypothesis are employed (See Appendix D). It must be stressed that the differences are between *groups* of firms, classified either as being involved in various ways with service bureaus or as not being involved in any way. Consequently, significant individual differences may be obscured in group data.

Office classification. Insofar as office classification is concerned, there do not appear to be significant differences between firms involved and those not involved with service bureaus. The proportion of involved and non-involved firms in each office classification is similar (See Table V-3). Therefore office classification (one-office or multi-office) and service bureau use appear unrelated.

TABLE V-3

OFFICE CLASSIFICATION OF RESPONDING CPA FIRMS

Service Bureau Relationship	Home Office	Branch	One Office Firm	Number Responding
Involved	10	9	42	61
Non-involved	9	5	47	61
Total	19	14	89	122

City size. The distribution of the involved firms over classes representing the size of the nearest large city does not differ significantly from the corresponding distribution of the non-involved firms.[5] The following inference, reflected in Table V-4, is statistically sound: proximity to cities large enough to support service bureaus is not a factor exerting strong influence over a CPA firm's relationship with them.[6] It should be noted, however, that substantial distances from cities large enough to support service bureaus may adversely affect a CPA-service bureau relationship. In fact, 10 percent of the non-involved firms are located in or near cities with fewer than 10,000 inhabitants; but distance apparently has not dissuaded several of the respondents from using service bureaus located hundreds of miles away. Many service bureaus specializing in accountants' packages customarily deal with geographically distant customers.

Of the 122 respondents to a question asking if the firm knew of a service bureau located within 20 miles, 25 firms indicated that they either did not know of one or that they were uncertain. Twenty of the 25 are non-involved firms, representing over 32 percent of all non-involved firms. Of the 20, one-half are located in or within 20 miles from cities with over 120,000 inhabitants, cities which have service bureaus. Nine of the 10 firms are located in or near cities with over 200,000 inhabitants.

TABLE V-4

RESPONDENT'S CITY SIZE OR SIZE OF LARGEST CITY WITHIN TWENTY MILES

Service Bureau Relationship	*Number of Inhabitants in Thousands*						Over 200	Number Responding
	Under 10	10- 20	20- 40	40- 80	80- 120	120- 200		
Involved	0	2	1	6	7	4	41	61
Non-involved	66	1	2	3	3	2	45	62
Total	6	3	3	9	10	6	86	123

Measures of size. Generally, the involved firms are larger than those non-involved firms by such measures as clients served, gross annual billings, and professional staff size.[7] In 1965, approximately 60 percent of the involved firms served more than 100 clients, while over 80 percent of the non-involved firms served less than 100 clients (see Table V-5). Similarly, almost 80 percent of the involved firms earned more than $50,000 while nearly two-thirds of the non-involved firms earned less than $50,000 (see Table V-6). Table V-7 contains certain measures of central tendency indicating that there are significant differences in professional staff size between the two categories of firms.

Although these significant differences exist, it should not be inferred that a service bureau relationship is a characteristic peculiar to larger firms only. In two measures of size employed, involved firms are found in classes representing the smallest of firms (see Tables V-5 and V-6). In the third measure, the distribution formed by the involved firms is very positively skewed, reflecting the strong influence of several very large firms (see Table V-7). Consequently, smaller firm size and service bureau involvement are not mutually exclusive.

Professional staff characteristics. Some significant differences in staff characteristics exist between the two categories of firms studied. Expressed as a percent of firms in a category, involved firms have staffs of higher quality in terms of the following characteristics than have the non-involved firms (See Table V-8):

TABLE V-5
DISTRIBUTION OF RESPONDENTS BY THE
NUMBER OF CLIENTS SERVED IN 1965

				Clients Served					Number
Service Bureau Relationship	Under 10	10-30	31-50	51-100	101-150	151-200	201-250	251-300	Over 300	Responding
Involved	1	4	8	10	14	6	5	0	13	61
Non-involved	3	18	18	13	6	3	1	0	0	62
Total	4	22	26	23	20	9	6	0	13	123

TABLE V-6
DISTRIBUTION OF RESPONDENTS BY 1965 BILLINGS

		Billings in Thousands					Number
Service Bureau Relationship	Less than $12	$12-$25	$25-$50	$50-$100	$100-$250	Over $250	Responding
Involved	1	4	7	16	15	18	61
Non-involved	9	19	14	16	4	0	62
Total	10	23	21	32	19	18	123

TABLE V-7
CENTRAL TENDENCY MEASURES OF
PROFESSIONAL STAFF SIZE

Measure	Involved Firms	Non-Involved Firms
Mean	17.1	2.4
Medium	6	2
Mode	4	1
Number responding	60	61

1. staff members spending half-time or more in management services[8]
2. staff members receiving 80 hours or more of formal electronic data-processing (EDP) training
3. staff members gaining systems and procedures experience[9]

In addition, a larger proportion of involved firms than those non-involved had college graduates on their staffs. This educational factor may well influence the characteristics enumerated above which are related to management services capabilities. Education, combined with experience, assists a CPA in attaining competence in the management services area.

TABLE V-8
PERCENTAGE OF FIRMS IN EACH CATEGORY EXHIBITING SELECTED STAFF CHARACTERISTICS

Staff Characteristics	Service Bureau Relationship	
	Involved	Non-Involved
With college degrees	85.0%	71.8%
Half-time or more in management services	21.7	4.9
Eighty hours or more of formal EDP training	20.0	3.3
Systems and procedures experience	65.0	36.1
Number responding	60	61

Client characteristics. Involved firms appear to render a different type of service than do the non-involved firms. Although the proportion of non-opinion audit clients appears approximately equal in both, involved firms have a larger proportion of clients preparing their own financial statements and a smaller proportion of write-up clients than have the non-involved firms (see Table V-9). In fact, 50 percent or more of the clients served by one-half of the non-involved firms represent bookkeeping engagements.

The measures in Table V-9 relating to non-opinion audit clients indicate that a rather substantial area of commonality exists in the practices of involved and non-involved firms. Almost 43 percent of the respondents, 24 involved and 28 non-involved firms, report non-opinion audit clients compose 45 percent or more of total clients served. However, of the non-involved firms in this group, one-third report they are not familiar with the capabilities and limitations of service bureaus. Therefore, it appears that non-involved firms whose practices resemble those of a large portion of involved firms cannot argue that their lack of a service bureau relationship stems from differences in the types of clients. A more convincing argument relates to an apparent lack of knowledge concerning service bureaus.

Management services activity. Management services activity is greater for the involved firms than for those non-involved.[10] More than one-half of the involved firms report management services billings constituted over 11 percent or more of 1965 gross billings; more than one-third of these indicate management services billings exceeded 20 percent of gross billings (see Table V-10). In contrast, almost 20 percent of the non-involved firms did not receive revenues from management services engagements in 1965 and an added 45 percent note that management services billings accounted for less than 5 percent of gross billings.

TABLE V-9
CENTRAL TENDENCY MEASURES OF CERTAIN CLIENT CHARACTERISTICS EXPRESSED AS A PERCENTAGE OF TOTAL CLIENTS

	Service Bureau Relationship					
Characteristics	*Involved*			*Non-Involved*		
	Mean	*Median*	*Mode*	*Mean*	*Median*	*Mode*
CPA performs write-up	25%	10%	10%	47%	50%	20%
Client performs bookkeeping and CPA prepares statements	37	25	10	39	33	50
Client prepares statements	38	20	0	14	0	0
Total	100%			100%		
Number responding	60			61		

TABLE V-10
BILLINGS FROM MANAGEMENT SERVICES ENGAGEMENTS AS A PERCENTAGE OF 1965 GROSS BILLINGS

Service Bureau Relationship		*Percentage of Gross Billings*							*Number Responding*
	None	*5% and Under*	*6-10%*	*11-15%*	*16-20%*	*21-25%*	*26-30%*	*30% Over*	
Involved	1	12	15	10	14	6	1	1	60
Non-involved	12	28	11	4	1	2	1	2	61
Total	13	40	26	14	15	8	2	3	121

Although statistically unsupported, it appears that management services engagements are becoming increasingly more important to involved firms than to their non-involved counterparts. Considering involved firms only, Table V-11 indicates that a larger proportion of these firms reports a relatively faster rate of increase in management services billings as compared to billings from all other services combined while a smaller proportion reports a comparatively slower rate of increase. This relationship is reversed for the non-involved firms.

Involved firms appear to receive more client requests for services related to EDP, such as computer feasibility studies and equipment selection, than do non-involved firms (see Table V-12).[11] Furthermore, these firms tend to service such requests themselves as compared with the non-involved firms (see Table V-13). Non-involved firms receiving EDP requests generally refer these to third parties.

Effects of electronic data processing. Involved firms display a more positive opinion with respect to the future effects of EDP, as

TABLE V-11

RATES OF CHANGE DURING RECENT YEARS OF MANAGEMENT SERVICES BILLINGS RELATIVE TO CHANGES IN BILLINGS FROM ALL OTHER SERVICES COMBINED

Service Bureau Relationship	Comparative Rate of Increase			Number Responding
	Faster	Slower	Equal	
Involved	21	4	33	58
Non-involved	3	15	32	50
Total	24	19	65	108

TABLE V-12

NUMBER OF CLIENT REQUESTS IN 1965 FOR SERVICES RELATED TO ELECTRONIC DATA PROCESSING

Service Bureau Relationship	Number of Requests						Number Responding
	None	1	2	3	4-15	Over 15	
Involved	18	14	5	3	14	6	60
Non-involved	48	8	4	1	0	0	61
Total	66	22	9	4	14	6	121

TABLE V-13

DISPOSITION OF CLIENT REQUESTS FOR SERVICES RELATED TO ELECTRONIC DATA PROCESSING

Service Bureau Relationship	(1) Number Receiving EDP Request	(2) Number Servicing Request Themselves	(2) ÷ (1)
Involved	42	34	80.9%
Non-involved	13	7	53.8%

TABLE V-14

OPINIONS RELATING TO THE FUTURE EFFECT OF ELECTRONIC DATA PROCESSING UPON THE ACCOUNTING PROFESSION AS COMPARED TO THE EFFECTS TO DATE

Service Bureau Relationship	Opinions						Number Responding
	Much Greater	Greater	About the Same	Less	Much Less	None	
Involved	32	22	7	0	0	0	61
Non-involved	12	33	12	1	1	2	61
Total	44	55	19	1	1	2	122

compared with the effects to date, than do the non-involved firms. As shown in Table V-14, a numerically and proportionately larger group of involved firms expect "much greater" relative future effects. Being involved to some extent with service bureaus, these firms may be in a better position to evaluate the future effects of EDP upon the profession than are the non-involved firms. Assuming that the non-involved firms are not as knowledgeable in these matters as are those involved, an example of self-deception may be contained in these statistics.

Sources of knowledge. Non-involved firms tend to acquire knowledge of service bureaus exclusively from secondary sources such as accounting literature and educational programs. Almost 88 percent of the non-involved firms did so as compared with less than 17 percent of the involved firms. This condition implies that secondary sources may be ineffective means of inspiring action compared to primary sources such as discussions with CPA users and service bureau representatives.

Expected effects of service bureau usage upon billings. Non-involved firms appear more pessimistic and unsure of the expected effects of service bureau usage upon gross billings.[12] It is shown in Table V-15 that over 40 percent of the non-involved firms fall into these categories as opposed to only 15 percent of the involved firms.

TABLE V-15

OPINIONS RELATED TO THE TENDENCY OF SERVICE
BUREAU USAGE TO REDUCE GROSS BILLINGS

Service Bureau Relationship	*Will Reduce*	*Opinions* *Uncertain*	*Will Not Reduce*	*Number Responding*
Involved	5	4	52	61
Non-involved	8	17	37	62
Total	13	21	89	123

Of the non-involved firms which believe that service bureau usage tends to reduce gross billings, 87.5 percent obtained their knowledge of such organizations from secondary sources only. Table V-16 illustrates this fact. This implies that secondary sources of information may foster relatively inaccurate impressions of service bureau costs and benefits as compared with primary sources.

TABLE V-16
EXCLUSIVE SOURCES OF SERVICE BUREAU KNOWLEDGE FOR NON-INVOLVED FIRMS, BY OPINION RELATING TO THE EFFECTS OF SERVICE BUREAU USAGE UPON BILLINGS

Source of Knowledge	Will Reduce	Opinions Will Not Reduce	Not Sure	Number Responding
Primary	1	27	7	35
Secondary	7	7	8	22
No response	0	3	2	5
Total	8	37	17	62

*Differences Between Categories of
CPA Firms Involved in Various
Ways with Service Bureaus*

The second hypothesis states that differences exist between categories of firms involved in various ways with service bureaus. Because of factors related to the number and the distribution of responses, the survey data do not lend themselves to a statistical testing of the hypothesis. Although statistical tests were not used, the data are examined because they suggest the existence of some differences and enable the development of a descriptive profile of various categories of firms. The differences suggested and profiles developed relate only to categories composed of respondents to the detailed questionnaire. The following categories of firms, hereafter referred to by their category number, are examined:

Category II—CPA firms with clients directly using service bureaus

Category III—CPA firms using outside service bureaus to service clients

Category IV—CPA firms in both Categories II and III

Category V—CPA firms using their own equipment to service clients

Office classification. It is suggested in Table V-17 that for some categories, office classification and the category of service bureau usage may be related. For example, 80 percent of the firms in Category III are one-office organizations. This is a reasonable condition because CPA firms directly using service bureaus are often small one-office firms automating their write-up and non-opinion audit engagements. In comparison, at least four of the eleven Category V firms are multi-office organizations. (Eight Category V firms responded to the detailed questionnaire while eleven did so for the post card questionnaire.) Hence the data reasonably suggest that large size, implied by multi-office status, and equipment ownership are related. One fact is quite clear: if one-office status implies a relatively small firm, small size does not preclude a service bureau relationship.

TABLE V-17

OFFICE CLASSIFICATION OF RESPONDING CPA FIRMS
INVOLVED IN VARIOUS WAYS WITH SERVICE BUREAUS

| Category | *Office Classification* | | *One-office Firm* | *Number Responding* |
	Home Office	*Branch*		
II	3	5	19	27
III	2	0	8	10
IV	2	3	11	16
V	3	1	4	8
Total	10	9	42	61

City size. Being located in or near a large city may influence the *nature* of a CPA firm's service bureau relationship. Category IV and V firms, who by definition seem more intensely involved with service bureaus, are found exclusively in cities with over 80,000 inhabitants (see Table V-18). The former may employ more approaches to service bureau use because of the availability of a number of service bureaus in larger cities. Category V firms may acquire equipment to service clients for some of the same reasons that service bureaus tend to concentrate in larger cities, i.e., the

TABLE V-18

INVOLVED RESPONDENT'S CITY SIZE OR SIZE OF
LARGEST CITY WITHIN TWENTY MILES

| Category | *Population in Thousands* | | | | | *Number Responding* |
	Under 40	*40- 80*	*80- 120*	*120- 200*	*Over 200*	
II	3	2	1	2	19	27
III	0	4	1	0	5	10
IV	0	0	2	2	12	16
V	0	0	3	0	5	8
Total	3	6	7	4	41	61

demand for such services is probably greater in larger cities than in smaller ones.

Measures of size. Notable differences exist between some categories of firms for certain measures of size. Considering the number of clients served during 1965, firms in Categories IV and V serving more than 300 clients account for 31.3 percent and 50 percent of their respective categories. In addition, at least one-half of the firms in each of these categories served more than 150 clients. Conversely, 62.9 percent of all firms in Category II and 90 percent of the firms in Category III served less than 150 clients for the same period (see Table V-19).

In 1965, 62.5 percent of all Category IV firms grossed more than $250,000. Category II and IV firms billing more than $250,000 accounted for 37.5 percent and 25.9 percent of their respective categories. In comparison, 60 percent of all firms in Category III earned less than $100,000 while at least 50 percent of the firms in other categories earned more than $100,000 (see Table V-20).

TABLE V-19
NUMBER OF CLIENTS SERVED BY
INVOLVED FIRMS, 1965

Category	*Under 50*	*51- 100*	*101- 150*	*151- 200*	*201- 300*	*Over 300*	*Number Responding*
II	5	6	6	4	2	4	27
III	4	0	5	0	1	0	10
IV	2	3	3	1	2	5	16
V	2	1	0	1	0	4	8
Total	13	10	14	6	5	13	61

Number of Clients

TABLE V-20
GROSS BILLINGS OF INVOLVED FIRMS, 1965

1965 Gross Billings in Thousands

Category	*Under $25*	*$25- $50*	*$50- $100*	*$100- $250*	*Over $250*	*Number Responding*
II	2	3	8	7	7	27
III	1	3	2	4	0	10
IV	0	1	5	4	6	16
V	2	0	1	0	5	8
Total	5	7	16	15	18	61

Differences in staff size appear to vary insignificantly between Category II and IV firms. Category V firms tend to be slightly larger than Category II and IV firms. Category III firms are the smallest (see Table V-21).

TABLE V-21
MEASURES OF CENTRAL TENDENCY RELATING TO STAFF SIZES OF INVOLVED FIRMS

	Measure		
Category	*Mean*	*Median*	*Number Responding*
II	18.1	6	27
III	5.6	6	9
IV	20.7	8	16
V	22.9	18	8
			—
			60

Professional staff characteristics. Striking staff differences appear to exist between some categories of firms. Category IV contains a greater proportion of firms with full-time management services staffs (see Table V-22). In addition, Categories IV and V are similar and considerably different from the other categories in terms of staff members spending half-time or more in management services. Considering only staff members with over 80 hours of formal EDP training, Category V firms represent the highest proportion of firms per category. This condition reflects a fringe benefit of equipment ownership.

TABLE V-22
PERCENTAGE OF FIRMS IN EACH USER CATEGORY EXHIBITING SELECTED STAFF CHARACTERISTICS

	Category			
Staff Characteristics	*II*	*III*	*IV*	*V*
Full-time in management services	15.4%	—	25.0%	12.5%
Half-time or more in management services	15.4%	11.1%	31.3%	37.5%
Eighty hours or more of formal EDP training	15.4%	—	18.8%	62.5%
Systems and procedures experience	57.7%	55.5%	81.2%	75.0%
Number responding	26	9	15	8

Categories IV and V contain a greater proportion of firms with systems and procedures experience than do Categories II and III even though the latter categories have a sizeable proportion of firms with such capabilities. However, it appears that, based on staff training, Category V firms as a group may be more competent than others to render assistance in conjunction with EDP systems.

Client characteristics. Write-up clients account for 10 percent or less of the number of clients served by 58 percent of all firms in Categories II, IV, and V; however, the practices of one-half of the firms in Category III are composed of 50 percent or more of such accounts (see Table V-23). For non-opinion audit clients and for clients preparing their own statements, it is obvious in Tables

TABLE V-23

DISTRIBUTION OF WRITE-UP CLIENTS AS
A PERCENTAGE OF TOTAL CLIENTS

Category	10% or less	11-30%	31-50%	51-70%	Over 70%	Number Responding
	Percentage of Total Clients					
II	17	6	1	2	1	27
III	3	0	2	1	4	10
IV	9	3	2	1	1	16
V	4	2	0	0	1	7
Total	33	11	5	4	7	60

V-24 and V-25 that Category II and IV firms are fairly well distributed over the entire range. Category V firms generally serve a small proportion of write-up and non-opinion audit clients while Category III firms appear to concentrate their services upon these types of clients. Table V-26 illustrates these differences in terms of the mean percentage for each user category.

The data imply that in terms of professional interest the engagements of firms in Categories II, IV, and V are similar and generally of a different type than those of firms in Category III. However, there appears to be a rather substantial area of similarity pertaining to non-opinion audit clients among firms in Categories II, III, and IV.

Management services activities. Category IV firms as a group receive a larger proportion of their total billings from management services engagements than do other categories of firms. Almost two-thirds of the firms in Category IV report management services billings accounted for 16 percent or more of 1965 gross billings (see Table V-27). Proportionately half as many firms in Category II

TABLE V-24
DISTRIBUTION OF NON-OPINION AUDIT CLIENTS
AS A PERCENTAGE OF TOTAL CLIENTS

Category	*Percentage of Total Clients*					
	10% or less	*11-30%*	*31-50%*	*51-70%*	*Over 70%*	*Number Responding*
II	9	5	2	2	9	27
III	5	0	2	1	2	10
IV	6	1	4	3	2	16
V	4	1	0	1	1	7
Total	24	7	8	7	14	60

TABLE V-25
DISTRIBUTION OF CLIENTS PREPARING THEIR OWN
FINANCIAL STATEMENTS AS A PERCENTAGE OF
TOTAL CLIENTS

Category	*Percentage of Total Clients*					
	10% or less	*11-30%*	*31-50%*	*51-70%*	*Over 70%*	*Number Responding*
II	10	4	1	3	9	27
III	7	2	1	0	0	10
IV	7	3	1	0	5	16
V	2	1	0	1	3	7
Total	26	10	3	4	17	60

TABLE V-26
MEAN OF SELECTED CLIENT CHARACTERISTICS
EXPRESSED AS A PERCENTAGE OF TOTAL
CLIENTS FOR EACH CATEGORY OF FIRMS

Client Characteristics	*Category*			
	II	*III*	*IV*	*V*
CPA performs write-up	16%	54%	24%	23%
Client posts and journalizes but CPA prepares statements	40	35	38	26
Client prepares statements	44	11	38	51
Total	100%	100%	100%	100%
Number responding	27	10	16	7

fall into this range; however, Category II firms dominate the 21 to 25 percent range while Category IV firms are concentrated in the 16 to 20 percent range. Management services billings appear somewhat less important to Category V firms and negligible to most firms in Category III.

TABLE V-27

BILLINGS FROM MANAGEMENT SERVICES AS A
PERCENTAGE OF 1965 GROSS BILLINGS

| | | | *Percentage of Gross Billings* | | | | |
Category	None	*Under* 5%	6- 10%	11- 15%	16- 20%	21- 25%	*Over* 25%	*Number Responding*
II	0	4	9	4	4	5	1	27
III	1	6	0	2	1	0	0	10
IV	0	2	0	4	9	0	1	16
V	0	0	6	0	0	1	0	7
Total	1	12	15	10	14	6	2	60

More than 62 percent of Category IV firms report a faster rate of increase in management services billings relative to billings from all other services combined (see Table V-28). These firms represent almost one-half of all firms answering in this manner. In addition, not one firm in Category IV reported a slower rate of increase in management services billings as compared to billings from all other services combined.

Category IV firms are contacted more frequently by their clients than are other categories of firms for assistance related to EDP (see Table V-29). It is surprising to find Category V firms less frequently approached, given their apparent staff training and experience in EDP-related matters. In response to a question inquiring into the most frequent approach taken for disposing of such client requests, over 70 percent of the firms in Category IV receiving such requests report their firm performed the service alone. In contrast, 50 percent or more of each of the other categories of firms receiving such requests turned to outside sources for assistance. Category III firms receive very few EDP-related service requests, reflecting in part the large portion of smaller clients apparently served by these firms.

Firms with clients directly using service bureaus. All firms in Categories II and IV and some firms in Category V have clients

TABLE V-28

RATE OF INCREASE DURING RECENT YEARS OF MANAGE-
MENT SERVICES BILLINGS RELATIVE TO INCREASES
IN BILLINGS FROM ALL OTHER SERVICES COMBINED

	Comparative Rate of Increase			
Category	Faster	Equal	Slower	Number Responding
II	6	18	3	27
III	2	6	1	9
IV	10	6	0	16
V	3	3	0	6
	—	—	—	—
Total	21	33	4	58

TABLE V-29

NUMBER OF CLIENT REQUESTS FOR SERVICES RELATED
TO ELECTRONIC DATA PROCESSING

Category	Number of Requests					
	None	1-2	3-5	6-15	Over 15	Number Responding
II	6	11	6	2	2	27
III	8	1	1	0	0	10
IV	2	5	4	1	4	16
V	2	2	2	1	0	7
	—	—	—	—	—	—
Total	18	19	13	4	6	60

directly using service bureaus without the CPA as an intermediary
in the data flow. (By definition, Category III firms are without
clients directly using service bureaus.) As developed in Chapter
IV, direct client usage of service bureaus generally assumes that
the client maintains a bookkeeping or accounting staff and that one
or both of the following conditions exist:

1. Clerical applications are automated and useful analyses are
   obtained as by-products.
2. Control applications for such areas as inventory or production
   are automated.

Table V-30 contains the distribution of applications sought by clients
directly using service bureaus.

Clients of Category IV firms appear to dominate each type of
application, often numerically and, with one exception, in proportion to the number of firms responding in each category. In addition,
the number of Category IV firms with clients in each of the more

TABLE V-30

TYPES OF APPLICATIONS USED BY CLIENTS DEALING
DIRECTLY WITH SERVICE BUREAUS

			Applications					
Category	*Program-ming*	*Systems and Proce-dures*	*Control of Opera-tions*	*Various Analyses*	*Financial Statement and Ledgers*	*Payroll*	*Billing*	*Number Respond-ing*
II	2	1	9	10	1	14	7	20
IV	5	4	6	10	5	8	7	11
V	1	0	2	3	2	3	2	4
Total	8	5	17	23	8	25	16	35

sophisticated applications classes is impressive, especially considering that these CPA firms were, with one exception, either singularly
responsible or shared responsibility with other parties for clients'
decisions to use service bureaus. In comparison, Category II firms
seem less actively involved as a group with clients' service bureau
usage: over 37 percent of these firms indicate that they were not
responsible for clients' decisions to use service bureaus. Three of
the four Category V firms contributing to the contents of Table V-30
report they were responsible, at least in part, for clients' decisions
pertaining to service bureau usage.

A measure of the importance direct client usage of service bureaus has for the responding CPA firms appears in Tables V-31 and
V-32. Generally, there are no significant differences between categories of firms. However, several Category II firms have a fairly
large proportion of clients using service bureaus and receive a sizeable
portion of gross billings from such clients. An approximation of the
productivity attributable to clients directly using service bureaus
appears in Tables V-31 and V-32. Eleven respondents report that
the proportion of billings is greater than the proportion of clients.
Only four firms find the reverse to be true.

The respondents were asked if systems and procedures modifications were necessary for any clients using service bureaus prior
to beginning such usage. Twenty-eight responded affirmatively (see
Table V-33). Of these firms, almost one-half performed all of the
work themselves (see Table V-34). Numerically, Category IV firms
appear most active; however, all of the Category V firms aware of
the need for modifications performed the work themselves.

TABLE V-31
NUMBER OF CLIENTS DIRECTLY USING SERVICE
BUREAUS AS A PERCENTAGE OF TOTAL CLIENTS

Category	*5% and Under*	*6-10%*	*11-15%*	*16-20%*	*21-25%*	*Number Responding*
			Percentage of Clients			
II	14	4	2	1	1	22
IV	8	4	0	0	0	12
V	5	0	0	0	0	5
Total	27	8	2	1	1	39

TABLE V-32
BILLINGS FROM CLIENTS DIRECTLY USING SERVICE
BUREAUS AS A PERCENTAGE OF TOTAL BILLINGS

Category	*5% and Under*	*6-10%*	*11-15%*	*16-20%*	*Over 20%*	*Number Responding*
			Percentage of Clients			
II	14	2	2	0	4	22
IV	7	4	1	0	0	12
V	2	1	0	0	0	3
Total	23	7	3	0	4	37

TABLE V-33
RESPONSES OF CPA FIRMS REPORTING ON THE NEED OF
SYSTEMS AND PROCEDURES MODIFICATIONS CAUSED
BY CLIENTS' SERVICE BUREAU USAGE

Category	*Needed*	*Not Needed*	*Not Sure*	*No Response*
		Responses		
II	13	6	3	5
IV	12	0	0	4
V	3	0	1	4
Total	28	6	4	13

TABLE V-34
DISPOSITION OF THE MODIFICATIONS NEEDED

Category	*All*	*Approximately Half*	*Less than Half*
	Portion of Modifications Performed by the CPA Firm		
II	3	3	2
IV	7	1	4
V	3	0	0
Total	13	4	6

CPA firms servicing clients through service bureaus. All firms in Categories III, IV, and V service clients through service bureaus, either an outside organization or one in which the CPA firm has a financial interest. Table V-35 presents the types of applications used by the 27 firms volunteering such information. The great majority use service bureaus for preparing financial statements and general ledgers. Except for payroll processing, it appears that analytical applications are next important in terms of use while control applications seem to be least important. If it is assumed that analyses are obtainable from processing related to clerical functions, then it appears not all firms are taking advantage of such a condition. With

TABLE V-35
SELECTED SERVICE BUREAU APPLICATIONS USED
BY CPA FIRMS FOR SERVICING CLIENTS THROUGH
SERVICE BUREAUS

	Financial State-ments and General Ledger	Pay-roll	Sales Analy-sis	Receiv-ables Aging	Tax Returns	Labor Distri-bution	Payables Distri-bution	Year End Inven-tory	Bill-ing	Con-trols	No. Re-spond-ing
Category					Applications						
III	8	3	2	2	2	0	2	0	0	0	10
IV	10	7	4	3	5	3	1	3	2	1	11
V	6	5	3	2	0	3	2	2	2	2	6
Total	24	15	9	7	7	6	5	5	4	3	27

15 firms using payroll applications, it is expected that an equal number should obtain labor distributions.

In terms of the overall sophistication of applications, Category V firms apparently out-perform all other categories. Category III firms concentrate upon clerically-oriented operations and very little upon analyses. Category IV firms cover the entire range of applications but apparently concentrate to a much lesser degree upon controls and analyses applications.

The importance of clients serviced through service bureaus for firms in Categories III, IV, and V is illustrated in Tables V-36 and V-37. Category III firms are heavily involved in servicing arrangements of this type. The productivity of these engagements for Category III firms is unmistakable: clients serviced in this way, expressed as a percentage range of total clients, are always equal to or less than billings expressed as a percentage range of total billings. One-third of the respondents from Categories III, IV, and V report the proportion of billings greater than the proportion of clients while only 11.1 percent indicate the reverse to be true.

Effects of electronic data processing. More than two-thirds of all Category IV firms express the belief that the effects of EDP upon the accounting profession over the next five years will be "much greater" than the effects to date. Category V firms seem similarly impressed with the future impact of EDP. Because these categories

TABLE V-36

NUMBER OF CLIENTS BEING SERVICED THROUGH A SERVICE BUREAU AS A PERCENTAGE OF TOTAL CLIENTS

Percentage of Clients

Category	5% and Under	6-10%	11-15%	16-20%	21-25%	26-30%	31-40%	41-50%	Over 50%	Number Responding
III	5	0	0	1	0	1	1	1	1	10
IV	5	2	1	1	1	0	0	0	1	11
V	1	2	1	1	0	0	0	0	1	6
Total	11	4	2	3	1	1	1	1	3	27

TABLE V-37

BILLINGS FROM CLIENTS SERVICED THROUGH A SERVICE BUREAU AS A PERCENTAGE OF TOTAL BILLINGS

Percentage of Billings

Category	5% and Under	6-10%	11-15%	16-20%	21-25%	26-30%	31-40%	41-50%	Over 50%	Number Responding
III	5	0	0	0	0	0	0	1	4	10
IV	3	4	2	0	0	0	0	0	2	11
V	0	3	0	1	0	1	0	0	1	6
Total	8	7	2	1	0	1	0	1	7	27

of firms appear more heavily involved with some form of EDP than other categories, their opinions reflect, in part at least, past decisions related to their present commitments (see Table V-38). It should be added that three Category IV firms report computers on order. Although no reasons were given for this course of action, it appears reasonable to assume that their experiences with service bureaus has had some effect on their decision.

Years of experience and benefits. Category IV firms lead all others in years of experience with service bureaus. As a group, these firms report an average of approximately five and one-half

TABLE V-38
OPINIONS RELATING TO THE FUTURE EFFECT OF ELECTRONIC DATA PROCESSING UPON THE ACCOUNTING PROFESSION AS COMPARED TO THE EFFECTS TO DATE

		Opinion		
Category	Much Greater	Greater	About the Same	Number Responding
II	12	11	4	27
III	4	4	2	10
IV	11	4	1	16
V	5	3	0	8
	—	—	—	—
Total	32	22	7	61

TABLE V-39
MEASURES OF THE NUMBER OF YEARS CLIENTS HAVE BEEN DIRECTLY USING SERVICE BUREAUS

	Measures[1]		
Category	Mean	Median	Number Responding
II	3.7	4	10
IV	5.6	6	11
V	3.6	4	7

[1]If clients had used service bureaus for over eight years, they were arbitrarily assumed to have used them for nine years. Only one Category III firm is affected by this assumption.

TABLE V-40
MEASURES OF THE NUMBER OF YEARS CLIENTS HAVE BEEN SERVICED THROUGH SERVICE BUREAUS

	Measures[1]		
Category	Mean	Median	Number Responding
III	4.1	3	22
IV	5.4	5	10
V	3.0	3	4

[1]If CPA firms had used service bureaus for over eight years, they were arbitrarily assumed to have used them for nine years. Three Category II and four Category III firms are affected by this assumption.

years of experience in servicing clients directly using service bureaus and in servicing clients through such organizations (see Tables V-39 and V-40). Considering this experience factor, it is noteworthy that Category IV firms report greater benefits from service bureau relationships than do other categories. As shown in Tables V-41 and

V-42, Category IV firms often account for the largest number of responses per benefit and for the largest proportion of firms per category reporting benefits.

TABLE V-41
SELECTED BENEFITS REPORTED BY FIRMS WITH CLIENTS DIRECTLY USING SERVICE BUREAUS, BY CATEGORY

	Number of Firms Reporting		
Benefits Reported	*II*	*IV*	*V*
Expanded services	0	5	3
Increased gross billings	0	0	1
Acquired more clients because of increased EDP proficiency	0	3	1
Number responding	21	10	4

TABLE V-42
SELECTED BENEFITS REPORTED BY FIRMS USING SERVICE BUREAUS TO SERVICE CLIENTS, BY CATEGORY

	Number of Firms Reporting		
Benefits Reported	*III*	*IV*	*V*
Staff trained in EDP	2	5	3
Increased number of clients	4	2	5
Fee structure higher	2	3	3
Work pace less hectic	6	5	4
Number responding	10	11	7

SERVICE BUREAU-COMMERCIAL
BANK QUESTIONNAIRE

The questionnaire sent to service bureaus and to certain commercial banks located in Michigan obtained information related to their activities and opinions (see Appendix C). The service bureaus were instructed in a cover letter to respond only if they offered commercial, as opposed to scientific, data processing services. Similarly, the banks were asked to respond only if they offered data processing services of the type clients of CPAs or CPAs themselves would find attractive (see Appendix C). Table V-43 presents the distribution of responses.

The number of responses to the survey should be evaluated in light of the instructions contained in the cover letters. Then, too,

TABLE V-43
PARTICIPATION IN THE SERVICE
BUREAU–COMMERCIAL BANK SURVEY

	Number Surveyed	Number Responding	Percent Responding
Service bureaus	64	23	35.9%
Commercial banks	50	16	32.0%
Total	114	39	34.2%

the method employed for selecting the service bureaus to be surveyed may well have included some organizations not offering commercial data processing services. In addition, service bureaus primarily performing commercial services such as the direct mailing of circulars may not have responded. In addition, not all of the 50 largest banks in Michigan are computerized and furthermore, of those that are, not all offer service bureau-type services.[13] For these reasons, all inferences drawn from the sample data are assumed to apply reliably to the population.

The equipment used by the respondents is summarized in Table V-44. The two banks not responding to the question which pertained

TABLE V-44
EQUIPMENT OPERATED BY THE RESPONDING SERVICE
BUREAUS AND COMMERCIAL BANKS

	Equipment Operated			No On-Premise Equipment	Number Responding
	Computer	Tab Equipment	Computer and Tab		
Service bureaus	9	3	11	0	23
Commercial banks	8	0	5	1	14
Total	17	3	16	1	37

to equipment ownership substantiate the earlier assertion that not all of the 50 largest Michigan commercial banks are computerized. However, one of these reported that by November of 1966 it would be equipped with an NCR 315 and would then offer data-processing services for customers. Neither bank offers computerized customer services through the facilities of a correspondent bank or service bureau and for that reason they are eliminated from further reference.

Servicing activities, in terms of the number of customers served, vary significantly between service bureaus and banks. In 1965, almost one-half of the responding service bureaus served more than 100 customers while, for the same period, almost 80 percent of the banks served fewer than 100 customers (see Table V-45). Nine banks had fewer than 50 customers while two banks reported servicing more than 500 customers.

TABLE V-45

CUSTOMERS SERVICED IN 1965

| | Customers Serviced | | | | | | | | | |
	10 and Under	10-25	26-50	51-100	101-200	201-300	301-400	401-500	Over 500	Number Responding
Service bureaus	2	4	2	4	5	2	0	0	4	23
Commercial banks	5	1	3	2	0	0	0	0	2	13
Total	7	5	5	6	5	2	0	0	6	36

Only seven service bureaus and three banks reported that direct CPA users were numerically important (over 20 percent of total customers served). Of these, three service bureaus and two banks served more than 50 customers. One of the service bureaus indicated that more than 40 percent of its 500 customers were direct CPA users. This particular organization specializes in accountants' packages on a national basis. A substantial number of respondents in both classes do not have direct CPA users while almost one-half of the service bureaus reported CPAs constituted 15 percent or less of their total number of customers (see Table V-46).

TABLE V-46

DIRECT CPA USERS AS A PERCENTAGE OF THE
NUMBER OF CUSTOMERS SERVED

| | Percentage Direct CPA Users | | | | | | | | |
	None	5% and Under	6-10%	11-15%	16-20%	21-25%	26-30%	31-40%	Over 40%	Total
Service bureaus	4	7	4	1	0	1	0	1	5	23
Commercial banks	5	0	0	1	0	0	1	0	2	9
Total	9	7	4	2	0	1	1	1	7	32

CPA referrals appear to be an insignificant proportion of the total customers served by the respondents (see Table V-47). This was especially true among banks. It may be that service bureaus and banks rely mainly upon their own marketing efforts. Further, it may reflect the extent of CPA firms' non-involvement with servicing organizations and a tendency on the part of service bureaus and banks to ignore CPA firms' close relationships with clients. There were some notable exceptions, however. Two banks, each with between 51 and 100 customers, reported that from 16 to 20 percent of their customers were CPA referrals. One of these banks had a substantial number of direct CPA users and offered a variety of data-processing applications. Two service bureaus each serving more than 50 customers also reported a sizable number of CPA referrals. These organizations also offered a wide variety of applications.

TABLE V-47

CPA REFERRALS AS A PERCENTAGE OF THE
NUMBER OF CUSTOMERS SERVED

		Percentage CPA Referrals							
	None	*5% and Under*	*6- 10%*	*11- 15%*	*16- 20%*	*21- 25%*	*26- 30%*	*31- 40%*	*Over 40%*	*Total*
Service bureaus	6	9	4	1	0	0	1	0	1	22
Commercial banks	8	3	0	0	2	0	0	0	0	13
Total	14	12	4	1	2	0	1	0	1	35

Almost 57 percent of the service bureaus and approximately 77 percent of the banks noted that the CPAs in each respondent's immediate marketing area were neither adequately apprised of nor knew how to use the data-processing services offered by the respondents (see Table V-48). Several of these respondents had a number of CPA users or referrals as customers. Involved as they are with CPAs, these respondents may be aware of a great untapped and possibly uninformed market for their services. Seven other respondents were in a sense more critical, indicating that CPAs were apprised of the services offered but did not know how to use them. Six service bureaus responding in this manner provided a rather wide selection of applications, especially the kind a CPA would recommend to a client needing a relatively sophisticated automated information system. This fact lends added reliability to their responses for the following reason: by marketing a variety of services, these respondents may have a better knowledge of their potential market than if they marketed a limited number of services only.

TABLE V-48

RESPONDENTS' EVALUATION OF THE EXTENT TO WHICH
CPAs ARE APPRISED OF AND KNOW HOW TO USE
DATA PROCESSING SERVICES

Respondents' Evaluations

	Yes, Very Much So	*Yes, Fairly So*	*No*	*Don't Know*	*Apprised of but Don't Know How to Use*	*Number Responding*
Service bureaus	0	2	13	2	6	23
Commercial bank	0	1	10	1	1	13
Total	0	3	23	3	7	36

From Table V-49 it appears that CPA firms receive little of the potentially lucrative systems set-up fees. Systems work is generally the only professionally interesting aspect of a service bureau involvement for most applications. The processing after the completion of the systems work usually requires relatively little expertise from the CPA.

TABLE V-49

PERFORMANCE OF MOST OF THE SYSTEMS WORK
ASSOCIATED WITH A DATA PROCESSING APPLICATION

Performance of the Systems Work

	Respondents Perform	*CPAs Perform*	*Divided Evenly Between CPAs and Respondents*	*Other Sources*	*Total*
Service bureaus	17	3	2	1	23
Commercial banks	9	0	1	0	10
Total	26	3	3	1	33

The CPA's reputation as a systems expert is subject to challenge (see Table V-50). Over 43 percent of the respondents who ventured an opinion were unflattering. Several of these had substantial contact with CPAs or with CPA referrals in terms of numbers or as a percentage of total customers. Most of these respondents offered a wide variety of services. The respondents expressing more favorable opinions had similar characteristics in terms of number of clients served, CPA users and referrals and services offered.

TABLE V-50

RESPONDENTS' OPINIONS OF THE CPA's PROFICIENCY AS A SYSTEMS MAN

| | *Proficiency Rating* | | | | | | | |
	Very Profi- cient	*Good*	*Fair*	*Poor*	*Very Poor*	*Don't Know*	*They Don't Perform Systems Work*	*Number Respond- ing*
Service bureaus	2	5	4	1	2	5	4	23
Commercial banks	0	1	1	1	0	7	2	12
Total	2	6	5	2	2	12	6	35

An indication of the extent CPAs are involved in systems work is revealed in the responses to the question "does your firm follow the practice of consulting with a customer's CPA firm for the first-time applications or modifications of existing ones?" The replies of the three respondents indicating that they never consult a CPA may be subject to question because they had relatively very few CPAs or CPA referrals as customers (see Table V-51). In addition, the three offer limited services. The remaining responses may indicate that CPAs are not uniformly involved in systems work and are possibly involved to a lesser degree than is commonly thought. Futhermore, certain negative control implications arise, assuming that some of the CPA referrals are opinion-audit clients, if in fact the CPA is not contacted when a client's system is modified.

TABLE V-51

THE EXTENT TO WHICH A CUSTOMER'S CPA FIRM IS CONTACTED FOR A NEW APPLICATION OR A MODIFICATION OF AN EXISTING APPLICATION

| | *Extent CPA Contacted* | | | | | |
	Always	*Usually*	*Some- times*	*Rarely*	*Never*	*Number Respond- ing*
Service bureaus	2	5	10	3	1	21
Commercial banks	1	3	2	2	2	10
Total	3	8	12	5	3	31

Similar unfavorable inferences may be drawn from the responses shown in Table V-52 to the question "do first-time CPA users of your services, or CPA's whose audit clients use your services for the first time, approach you about the controls in your processing prior to such use?" The respondents who indicated that they were never approached about controls dealt with a numerically small number of CPAs or CPA referrals and offered a limited range of services. However, the respondents who reported that "very few" or "some" CPAs approached them had substantial CPA contacts and offered a wide range of services. On the other hand, the respondents indicating that "all" CPAs approached them for information on internal controls had limited contacts with CPAs or CPA referrals and offered a limited range of services.

TABLE V-52
PROPORTION OF CPAs REQUIRING INFORMATION ON SERVICE BUREAU PROCESSING CONTROLS

	All	Most	Some	Very Few	Question Never Arose	Total
			Proportion			
Service bureaus	2	8	6	4	3	23
Commercial banks	1	0	2	4	5	12
Total	3	8	8	8	8	35

TABLE V-53
TYPE OF ASSISTANCE OR TRAINING SERVICES OFFERED CUSTOMERS

	Formal Training	Informal Assistance	Training and Assistance	None	Total
		Type of Services Offered			
Service bureaus	3	14	3	2	22
Commercial banks	1	6	0	5	12
Total	4	20	3	7	34

It appears in Table V-53 that relatively few service bureaus or commercial banks offer formal training for their customers. However, informal assistance seems readily available.

The services offered by service bureaus and commercial banks are shown in Table V-54. The most popular service bureau applications appear to be payroll and various analyses followed closely by billing, various control applications, custom-designed systems, and programming. As expected, banks heavily favor payroll applications. However, one-half of them provide analytical applications and billing services. It is noteworthy that several banks offer programming assistance, custom-designed systems, and control applications.

TABLE V-54
SERVICES OFFERED BY RESPONDENTS

	Service Bureaus		Commercial Banks	
Services Offered	*Number Offering*	*Percent of Class*	*Number Offering*	*Percent of Class*
Equipment usage	10	43.5%	3	21.1%
Programming	19	82.6	5	35.7
Custom systems design and installation	20	87.0	5	35.7
General ledger and financial statements	19	82.6	2	14.3
Tax returns	7	30.0	0	—
Payroll	19	82.6	12	85.7
Various analyses (sales, receivables aging, etc.)	21	91.3	7	50.0
Various control applications (production, inventory, etc.)	19	82.6	6	42.9
Billing	19	82.6	7	50.0
Operation research	8	34.8	1	7.1
Scientific applications	7	30.0	0	—
Number responding	23		14	

Of special interest to CPAs is the fact that fourteen respondents (six service bureaus and eight banks) provide many of the services listed in Table V-54 to non-computerized banks, which in turn offer these to their customers. The majority of these respondents provided a wide selection of services. The implication is that CPAs concerned about the competitive effects of customer services rendered by computerized banks should also consider the data-processing capabilities of non-computerized banks with computerized correspondents or with neighboring service bureaus.

CONCLUSIONS

Given the information provided by the post card questionnaire and the number of CPA firms practicing in Michigan, the most optimistic measure indicates that approximately 40 percent of all practicing Michigan CPA firms are not involved with service bureaus. The most pessimistic measure places the proportion of non-involved firms at over 55 percent of the total. Although service bureaus are not of uniform quality and of universal applicability or without suitable alternatives, these organizations represent a versatile tool if properly selected, applied, and controlled. Hence, the statistics reflecting the non-involvement of CPA firms create concern because the profession in general may be ignoring a useful alternative for providing better services to many clients.

The data from the detailed questionnaire suggest CPA firms' service bureau involvements are substantially unaffected by such factors as single- or multi-office status, proximity to large cities, composition of a practice in terms of client characteristics, number of clients served, and even professional staff size. Although certain factors related to size appear more common to involved firms than to those non-involved, neither is the causality clear nor is it safe to infer that small size and service bureau involvements are mutually exclusive. In fact, a number of smaller CPA firms are involved to a greater extent than many larger organizations. However, it does appear that lack of knowledge and inaccurate information create misleading impressions and lead firms to conclude that relationships with service bureaus benefit neither the firm nor the clients.

Involved firms seem to find management services engagements more important to their practices than do the non-involved firms. Staff quality in terms of capabilities and training is higher for involved firms than for those non-involved. Similarly, data pertaining to client characteristics suggest that a greater proportion of engagements more professional in nature are found with involved firms than with their non-involved counterparts.

The examination of the involved CPA firms' responses suggests that firms more intensively involved with service bureaus exhibit certain attributes more often than do less intensively involved firms. For example, management services activities, staff quality, and the proportion of non-bookkeeping-type engagements is greater for firms more intensively involved than for others less involved. In addition, intensively involved firms work most frequently with the more sophisticated types of service bureau applications such as analyses and controls while the other firms appear to concentrate on bookkeeping or clerically oriented applications. Similarly, reported benefits from service bureau usage came primarily from the intensively involved firms.

The analysis of the involved firms' responses was not subjected to statistical tests. Consequently, inferences drawn from such data require qualification. Furthermore, it is not intended to imply that service bureau usage is causally related to the favorable attributes mentioned. Additional research is needed to prove or disprove any such relationship. However, it seems reasonable to suggest that service bureau usage may be an added favorable attribute of progressive CPA firms.

The responses of a sample of service bureaus and commercial banks, the latter offering service bureau-type services, substantiate the responses obtained from the CPA firms. For example, relatively few service organizations report a substantial amount of close and active relationships with CPA firms. In fact, the general tenor of these responses are uncomplimentary to the accounting profession and suggest that the following may be true:

1. CPA firms are uninformed of the services available from service bureaus.
2. CPA firms are not actively involved in systems work to the extent commonly assumed.
3. CPA firms are neglecting data control and reliability implications inherent in clients' use of off-premises servicing arrangements.
4. CPA firms are being by-passed during the systems installation and modification phases of their clients' service bureau applications.

Service organizations offer a wide range of applications. Of some surprise is the extent to which banks report offering such services as programming assistance and custom-designed systems. A substantial number of service bureaus and banks offer a variety of services through non-computerized banks which in turn offer these services to their customers. CPAs worried about the competitive influence of banks may have a basis for their concern. However, a progessive firm should consider the services rendered by these organizations as potentially beneficial to the firm and to its clients.

Finally, it should be stated that survey data collected from primarily objective-type questionnaires are subject to some qualification on the basis that ambiguity often exists whenever ideas are conveyed without the elucidating benefits of personal contact. Because of this obstacle, each of the questionnaires used was pretested and criticized by CPAs in public practice and in academic institutions, by service bureau representatives, and by a trained psychologist.

VI

Emerging Developments in the
Service Bureau Concept

The analysis of past and current conditions is often useful only as a vague guide for future action. In order that this action may be constructive, it is essential to recognize emerging developments and to relate these to past and current conditions. Two such developments in the service bureau concept are computerized commercial banks and multiple-access-computer service bureaus. These organizations, which reflect the challenge of information technology, may have very significant effects upon the future practice of public accounting.

Computerized Commercial Banks

The growth of automation in commercial banking was reviewed in Chapter II. In this chapter I examine the reasons banks computerize, their approaches to automation, their commercial computer services, the emerging trends in computerized customer services, and the implications of these considerations for the public accounting profession. The concept of an automatic credit transfer system,

---

The material in this chapter dealing with commercial banks has been published, in a revised form, in the Spring, 1967, issue of *The Ohio CPA*. The material pertaining to Multiple-Access-Computer Service Bureaus appeared, in slightly different form, in the March, 1968, issue of *Management Accounting*.

where in the long run the banking industry may emerge as a national financial information system, is briefly reviewed in the following section. Excluded from this study is pending legislation which would limit the extension of certain banking services.

Reasons for Using Computers

Commercial banks cite several reasons for using computers. Among these are the reduction of operating costs, the improvement of management information, and the development of a new source of revenues.

Reducing operating costs. Increased demand deposit activity and the trend to smaller corporate cash balances are important factors in the automation decisions of many banks. Computers were originally considered only as a means for lowering the operating costs associated with demand deposits and other clerically demanding applications such as savings deposits, instalment loans, and trusts. At the outset it appears that banks imitated the narrow computer perspective of their non-financial counterparts. Often there were no quantitative standards to support decisions to automate nor were there adequate qualitative standards to guide system design.[1]

Improving management information. In recent years, commercial banks have generally expanded the scope of their computerized applications into two new areas. One is the improvement of management information. While not as publicized as the second area, that of developing a new source of revenues, banks recognize that improved management information manifests itself in optimal resource utilization through better and timelier decisions.

In conjunction with the control aspects of computerized management information systems, some of the largest banks use operations research methods to enhance the planning necessary for sound decision making. These methods are applied to such areas as portfolio management, risk analysis of loan applications, statistical forecasting of economic conditions, and market research. Some examples of operations research applications are linear programming for determining the optimal mix of assets given the condition of the money and capital markets, and queuing theory for assisting in estimating the number of tellers needed during various hours of the day.

Developing a new source of revenues. Commercial banks as a group are aggressively marketing a variety of computer services to customers, services often identical to those offered by service bureaus. The profit potential associated with this new source of revenues is apparently a very important factor in the future automation plans of many banks. Neal J. Dean of Booz, Allen and Hamilton succinctly expressed that importance:

> There are by now many bankers who believe that the opportunity to develop a profit center through the sale of computer services is likely to prove the most significant of the three automation opportunities. Bankers who have developed well-defined programs for customer services envision a profit impact of the general magnitude of a well-run trust department. In other words, customer services could make contributions through a net fee income of at least 10 percent to 15 percent of the bank's net operating earnings, in addition to providing new business values and helping to retain balances.[2]

Many bankers strongly feel that many of these services are natural extensions of their traditional functions. Furthermore, many have expressed the opinion that computerized customer services cannot be allowed to go the way of instalment lending and term loans. At their inception, these services were not actively marketed and as a result banks have continuously experienced fierce competition from instalment loan houses and life insurance companies.

Approaches to Computer Usage

When the reasons for computerizing a bank's applications are sufficiently convincing, several alternative approaches exist. Among these are:

1. Acquiring an in-house installation
2. Organizing a computer cooperative with other banks
3. Sharing a non-financial commercial organization's facilities
4. Receiving services from a computer-owning correspondent
5. Using a service bureau

The advantages and disadvantages of each approach are beyond the scope of this study. Factors peculiar to a bank, such as its size, aggressiveness, location, and attitude toward independence influence the approach selected. Of equal importance are such factors as the cost of an owned installation as compared to the cost, services, proficiency, and proximity of an off-premises servicing arrangement.

According to a 1964 automation study performed by the American Bankers Association (ABA), 348 banks had on-premises computer installations while 226 used some type of servicing arrangement.[3] Over 80 percent of the banks installing their own computer had assets of over \$50 million, while more than 85 percent of the banks with a computer servicing arrangement were in the under \$50 million asset class.[4] The latter group's use of servicing arrangements is depicted in Table VI-1.

It should be noted that of the banks using an outside servicing arrangement, the smaller banks appear to rely on their computerized correspondents while the larger ones tend to use service bureaus,

TABLE VI-1
TYPE OF SERVICE ARRANGEMENT
(by asset size of bank in millions)

			Asset Size			
Arrangement	All Banks	Under $10	$10 to $50	$50 to $100	$100 to $500	$500 and Over
Correspondent bank	40%	51%	36%	21%	22%	100%
Service bureau	28	23	31	42	11	—
Joint venture with other bank	12	8	10	27	45	—
Computer servicing arrangement (non-banks)	3	1	5	5	—	—
Other	17	17	18	5	22	—
Total	100%	100%	100%	100%	100%	100%
Base	226	88	108	19	9	2

Source: Dale L. Reistad, "The Impact of Automation on the Nation's Banks," *Banking* (November, 1964), p. 107.

bank computer cooperatives, and non-bank sources primarily. Such a condition may indicate that larger non-computerized banks do not prefer service agreements with large computerized correspondents due to compensatory balance requirements or to the possible release of confidential information.

Computerized Customer Services

In 1964, the ABA announced that the banking industry was then installing computers at the rate of 200 systems per year.[5] Davies noted that of 13,000 banks surveyed by the ABA, 800 used computers. However, by 1975, the number is expected to increase to 6000.[6] Obviously, the rate of systems installation is increasing. Although banks initially concentrate on internal applications, the promise of new sources of revenues invariably finds them offering computerized customer services within two years of computer installation, often before most internal functions have been automated.[7] The statistics quoted indicate that these services will continue to grow and provide revenues through:

1. Fees charged for processing customers' applications
2. Additional services which the new customers may require
3. New balances maintained by these customers in conjunction with processing and additional services

The market for computerized customer services includes financial institutions, individuals, and businesses.

Financial institutions. Correspondent banks are the most commonly served financial institutions. A correspondent receives some of the internal data-processing applications a computerized bank performs for itself, such as demand and savings deposit accounting, instalment loans, and payroll. Automated accounting services for mortgage companies, savings and loan associations, and other financial institutions are also available. As a bank becomes more experienced in processing its own internal applications, servicing other financial institutions comes as a logical first step into the field of computerized customer services.

Individuals. Services for individuals include account reconciliation, paying agent services, and more recently credit card privileges. While these services have a comparatively limited potential for fee income, they promote additional services and provide new balances.

Businesses. During the 1964 ABA Automation Conference, Dean commented on computerized services for business customers as follows:

If we may judge the successes thus far attained, and more importantly, from the plans being made, it is possible that data processing volumes arising from. . . [services to business customers] . . . may eventually equal or exceed the volumes and the net fee income obtained from financial institutions.[8]

As originally conceived and implemented, these services were related to the traditional banking functions. Some of the earliest processing services offered were package programs for payroll, billing, accounts receivable, and account reconciliation. Remuneration was influenced by a management philosophy which emphasized overall bank profit ability and compensating balances rather than demanding that each service stand on its own.[9]

Today, the philosophy of rendering computerized services to each customer class is undergoing profound change. In the first place, banks are adopting marketing techniques for selecting the services to be offered. Customers' needs are evaluated, the market size is determined, and the potential market share is estimated. Secondly, a fee is established for each service which will recoup all operating costs as well as provide an element of profit. In an age when corporate comptrollers are becoming adroit cash managers, many banks are finding that given the choice between maintaining compensatory balances or paying a service charge which fails to cover all costs, customers tend to select the latter alternative. In addition, the current attention accorded management information systems causes many offices to recognize that computerized customer services are no longer justifiable solely on the basis of excess machine capacity. In fact, for many banks, excess machine capacity is a myth. A true management information system requires the automation of many internal functions which are now performed manually. These functions compete with customer services for available computer capacity. Internal applications are usually given priority. New equipment is added only if the customer services contemplated have a relatively riskless return, attractive in terms of size and recovery time of investment.

Generally, bank offerings of computerized services for business customers include the following:

1. payroll accounting
2. professional billing
3. lock box plans
4. account reconciliation
5. corporate trust services
6. bill collection for utilities

Clearly, these services are related to the basic banking functions of marketing and transferring credit. Professional billing services, for example, are based on the rationale that over 90 percent of all financial transactions today are consummated by means of checks and that an account balance is a prerequisite for entering into such a transaction. Consequently the processing steps associated with preparing and mailing statements, collecting remittances through lock box plans, preparing aging schedules, and financing receivables are considered as logical services for medical professionals who maintain a bank balance and receive check payments from patients. In a similar vein, George W. Mitchell made the following observation:

> It seems logical and practical that at least some of the customer accounting antecedent and subsequent to settlement could be most economically done in a coordinated package with the settlement accounting. Every sales transaction, for example, by specifying a settlement date, might immediately be put into the bank's computer where it could accomplish immediate settlement or subsequent reminder and settlement. Similarly, a bank could handle payrolls and agree to bill and process many types of contractual payments for insurance, rent, and mortgage payments. In short, by virtue of its central position in the payments process the bank is also able to perform ancillary and antecedent accounting and billing operations more economically than anyone else.[10]

The Trend in Computerized Services for Businesses

In the past, banks often offered computerized services to businesses in order to remain competitive with other banks. The prevailing attitude emphasized the deposit balance-generating aspects of such services rather than their profitability. Some banks were so intent upon offering computerized services to businesses that they went well beyond the applications associated with traditional banking functions into ". . . production planning, inventory control, etc., or . . . offered services which they [had] neither the expertise nor the equipment to provide."[11] Added to the competition from other banks was that from established service bureaus. Compared to the average service bureau, most computerized banks lacked depth in their systems and programming abilities and in their marketing efforts. It was soon evident that computerized services for businesses required a systems and programming staff with broad inter-industry experience and vast technical skill. In addition, the marketing effort was substantially different from that needed to attract correspondent bank business. One result for many banks was an unprofitable operation. This was especially true for those who engaged in price competition or who subscribed to the fallacy that increased profitability automatically results from the increased deposit balances provided by businesses receiving computerized services.

Generally, the banks which were successful in marketing computerized services to their business customers did so on a selective basis, beginning with and remaining close to those applications related to basic banking functions. Today, this wisdom appears to permeate the industry. The literature is replete with comments relating to the philosophy of computerized services for businesses which weigh the relative merits of a full service bureau approach versus the utilization of unused computer time or of deposit-oriented services versus all types of services. In the literature, the apparent consensus is aptly expressed by M. B. Basson of Price, Waterhouse and Company:

It seems to me that what [banks] are after is a natural, logical growth and an extension of services that are directly or tangentially involved with banking functions. I do not believe that [banks] are after a whole range of data processing services, such as might be offered by a commercially operating service bureau.[12]

Although the banking industry's members assert that their expanding offerings of computerized services will remain related to basic banking functions, it appears that these are a starting point only. In part, this may be due to the expanding nature of the banking function itself; however, it is submitted that competition from other banks and the profit potential inherent in such services are important motives. Davies notes that several banks are believed to generate over $1 million a year from computerized customer services.[13]

It appears that an increasing number of banks resemble commercial service bureaus in terms of the services offered. For example the Automated Accounting Center of Connecticut, a division of the Waterbury National Bank, offers over 20 package program services, among which are the following:

1. general ledger accounting
2. cost distributions
3. invoicing
4. statistical summaries
5. inventory control
6. engineering calculations
7. statistical inventory forecasting
8. sales analysis and commission calculation
9. managerial control reports

The center serves professional accountants, industrial wholesalers, small to medium manufacturers, chain retail food stores, restaurants, and small service organizations, among others.

The apparent inconsistency between much of the literature and practice, which parallels the debate in accounting circles relative to the scope of management services, is further reflected in the commentary of Arthur S. Kranzley. Tracing the development of bank automation, he notes that the dilemma of the bank as a service bureau versus traditional banking roles is being resolved. Bankers recognize that ". . . customers want this information processing capability—but want it applied to enhancement of existing services and to financial services which accelerate and expand the acquisition and placement of funds."[14] The ambiguity increases as Kranzley asserts the following:

Business accounts . . . stand in need of financial services which will extend working capital to the maximum degree with minimum risk. For example, the commercial bank offering a sophisticated inventory control system and parallel financing on inventories so controlled is offering a financial service which allows a new level of entrepreneurial freedom.[15]

If bankers are resolving their dilemma thus, then one could rationalize the propriety of offering scentific data-processing services in conjunction with a term loan for research and development purposes. Therefore, it is submitted that as banks gain more expertise, experience additional competition, and recognize profitable markets, they will expand the volume and scope of their computerized business services. Their probability of success is enhanced by their established relationships with the business community, ample capital for equipment and personnel, and an increasingly aggressive attitude toward profits.

In Chapter V, it was noted that at least 14 of the 50 largest commercial banks in Michigan offer computerized services to business. Table VI-2 summarizes their reported offerings.

As expected, payroll and billing services are most commonly offered. These are clearly related to traditional banking functions. Analytical services associated with receivables, payables, and payroll are indirectly related to these functions. However, control applications for such areas as inventory and production are more remotely related to traditional banking functions. At this point it is difficult to differentiate a bank's offerings from those of a commercial service bureau. Finally, when a significant number of respondents indicate they offer such technical services as custom-designed systems and programming assistance, the assertion that future bank services will

TABLE VI-2
COMPUTERIZED CUSTOMER SERVICES
OFFERED BY FOURTEEN MICHIGAN
COMMERCIAL BANKS

Service Description	Number Offering Service
Payroll	12
Billing	7
Various analyses such as sales and receivables aging	7
Various control applications such as production and inventory control	6
Custom systems design and installation	6
Programming assistance	5
Equipment usage by customers' personnel	3
General ledger and financial statements	2
Operations research applications such as PERT	1
Other	6

Source: Data compiled from questionnaire.

remain oriented to traditional functions is subject to challenge. For one thing, once a service is offered it is often unwise, from a competitive standpoint, to terminate it. And as competitors innovate, it is often necessary to imitate them.

In their 1964 study, the ABA noted that about 20 percent of the computerized respondent banks offered automated services of some type to their customers.[16] These services were offered most frequently by the larger banks.[17] In a 1965 survey, NABAC, the Association for Bank Audit, Control and Operation, reported that almost 50 percent of the respondents from a sample of 430 computerized banks offered accounting services to customers.[18] As defined by NABAC, these services included billing, accounts receivable, credit card accounting, payroll, and preparation of tax records. As did the earlier ABA study, the NABAC study indicated that a substantial number of banks were soon planning to offer computerized customer services.

Of eighteen common computer applications, NABAC found that only four applications were more often automated than commercial or business customer services. These were the internal applications of demand and savings deposits, payroll, and instalment loans. Of even greater significance in the NABAC study were the responses to a question which solicited opinions regarding the degree of importance to banking of 13 general application areas over the ensuing five-year period. The importance ascribed to each application is reflected in the ranking accorded them. In terms of the total degree of importance to the banking industry, the ranking was as follows:

1. Accounting services for business customers
2. Accounting services for correspondent banks
3. Automated management information records
4. Analysis services for business customers
5. Data transmission—local/bank to bank
6. Data transmission—long distances
7. Personal customer services
8. Analysis and operations research for correspondent banks
9. Data transmission—local/bank to customer
10. Operations research for business customers
11. Automated credit records—local
12. Modeling or stimulation
13. Automated credit records—nationwide

Two factors appear obvious. One is the high ranking accorded accounting and analysis services for business customers. Second, by considering analysis and operations research services for business customers as separate categories, the banking industry may be contemplating expanded offerings of such services. It is important in itself that operations research for business customers was a separate category.

The Implication of Bank Computer
Services for the Accounting Profession

Many expressions of concern have been voiced within the accounting profession over the entrance of banks into the business of offering service bureau-type services. What apparently originated as rental of excess computer time has evolved into a group of basic data processing services for customers. CPAs with a large part of their practices devoted to write-up engagements are especially concerned. They realize that banks, unlike service bureaus, have an established relationship with the business community. Furthermore, banks are not ethically constrained from soliciting customers. From the standpoint of the overall profession, however, banks are merely extending the existing services provided by service bureaus.[19] As such,

the enlightened CPA should accept this trend as a relief rather than a menace. He can rid himself of the drudgery of routine bookkeeping, show his clients how to benefit from automation, and spend his time to greater advantage by giving his clients services of a more professional and sophisticated character.[20]

It appears that the banking industry is presenting the accounting profession a subtle challenge, even greater than that previously mentioned. Today, the banks are offering package processing services for financial statements, inventory control, insurance, taxes, sales analyses, and debt management; tomorrow they may become a financial advisory service for their customers.[21] The banking literature has numerous references to financial advisory services which banks are considered qualified to perform. The services are viewed as natural extensions of banking functions. However, it is submitted that many of these services, which differentiate a bank from and allow it to compete effectively with a service bureau, resemble those performed by CPAs. Furthermore, the indications are that these services will extend beyond financial advice. For example, 9 of the 14 Michigan banks offering computerized customer services perform most of the systems work required to process a customer's application. As banks become more proficient in establishing their own management information system, it is expected that they will expand the scope of such services. This is the real challenge posed by the present computerized record-keeping services of banks.

It has been noted that the attest function may also be in jeopardy or that at least it should be re-examined if banks perform all or most of the data processing for clients of CPAs. If banks maintain and prepare a client's records, the need for many certified reports may vanish. For example, the bank can use the data stored in the memory of its computer to analyze the desirability of granting a loan. The following may be readily available or obtained with a minimum of computer time:

1. the status of the aged receivables
2. the seasonal sales peaks and valleys
3. the loan applicant's collection habits
4. the inventory turnover
5. the payment practices of the loan applicant[22]

Then by using operations research techniques, trends and forecasts can be prepared. How many certified reports provide such information? Of course, there are many factors to challenge this anticipation, as for instance: How many clients would welcome such an arrangement with a credit grantor? Would the bank perform the audit field work? In addition, this situation requires an examination of factors similar to those encountered when clients use service bureaus. The bank's records and system of control may fall within the scope of the audit.

It is submitted that the challenge of bank computer services can be effectively met by the accounting profession in a manner identical to that prescribed for meeting the challenge of commercial service bureaus. The CPA should recommend to his clients the services of banks offering quality computerized services. This would reduce much of the time-consuming manual operations the CPA performs. Then, he should concentrate upon further developing his financial advisory skills and his systems capabilities. In this manner, the CPA will reserve for himself the key advisory role which his training and experience qualify him to occupy.[23]

The Multiple-Access-Computer Service Bureau

The second new development in the service bureau concept is the advent of multiple-access-computer service bureaus. Service bureaus such as these provide computer users a high degree of machine responsiveness. Consequently, a true management information system becomes a distinct possibility in the foreseeable future for firms unable to justify economically their own computer but who could benefit from a computer's capabilities. In fact, multiple-access-computer service bureaus offer advantages for many firms which currently maintain their own computers.

The multiple-access-computer service bureau is an application of the concept termed "time-sharing." To better appreciate the potential of multiple-access-computer (MAC) service bureaus, "time-sharing," the characteristics of MAC service bureaus, the type currently in existence and those projected for the future and the implications of MAC service bureaus for the accounting profession are briefly considered in this section.

Time-Sharing

Time-sharing can be non-technically described as the simultaneous use of a computer by a number of users. However, the idea of sharing a computer is not new and for that reason the term "time-sharing," as it relates to MAC service bureaus, is misleading.[24] Today, departments within a firm share a computer. Each department usually has a specified block of time available wherein like transactions are grouped and processed in definable batches. Implicit in such operations are the inconveniences of waiting until a specified time, processing for a given time-period only, updating records periodically, and producing documents which reflect randomly occurring events without concern for their relative time dimensions. Another form of sharing a computer is in the use of a service bureau. Basically, the operations are similar to that of an on-premises computer installation. The same inconvience exists, usually with the addition of a greater geographic distance between user and computer.

The relatively recent interjection of data communications devices between a computer and its users removes the inconvenience of transporting the processable data to the computer installation. On-premises installations, service bureaus, and computerized banks use several types of data communications devices in conjunction with batch-processing computer services. But the data must often be transmitted at specified times while processed information may be returned by mail, messenger, etc.

In contrast, time-sharing is a very responsive concept which stresses the importance of the interaction between a computer and its users. By means of an on-premises console, each user finds that the computer is immediately accessible, providing instantaneous responses to requests for information, preparation of documents, design of new programs, and a variety of other functions. Time-sharing seeks to maximize the inherent efficiency in man-machine collaboration by allowing each to perform that part of a task for which he or it is best qualified. Man is best suited for providing judgment in handling exceptions and for recognizing overall trends and implications; the computer excels in performing computations, file retrieval, and other such operations.[25]

Another important aspect of time-sharing is its cost as it relates to computer size. Time-sharing seeks to solve the following situation described by Charles W. Adams:

To work economically with a man in a system where each waits in turn for the other, the computer should presumably have an hourly cost about the same as that of the man. But the economics of computers, like those of any automatic production process, imply a rapid reduction in price per computation as the volume of computation increases. While computers are available in the $20,000 price range, making them comparable in monthly rental to the salary of a competent clerk or service engineer, they are small, slow machines severely limited in storage capacity and input-output versatility. By paying ten times as much for a computer, one gets much more than ten times the computing power; and by paying a hundred times as much, one gets an even greater increase. Meanwhile, the gap between the rental of the machine and the salary of the man is widening at an alarming rate. Thus it seems clear that much can be gained by sharing one computer among many users.[26]

The operations of a time-shared system are quite complex. Under the control of a special executive program, each user is polled many times a second in order to determine if a service request exists. When a request arrives, its nature is determined and the executive program selects from the user's list of programs the proper one to perform the processing. Simultaneously, polling of other users continues. If another request arrives and is of a higher priority, or if the currently operating program needs to use a peripheral device and thus temporarily terminates its need for the computer's arithmetic and logic unit, the currently operating program is interrupted. The step attained in the program and the interim results are stored while the next program is started. Polling continues and a queue of waiting service requests is the system's normal state.

Usually, after a specified processing time has elapsed, say one-fiftieth of a second, an incomplete job is interrupted and temporarily stored so that other users may be serviced. The executive program continually moves programs in and out of the arithmetic and logic unit in order that that unit be fully utilized at all times. Clearly, this arrangement provides for the practically uninterrupted use of the computer's computational power. Thus a highly sophisticated computer becomes economically feasible, as it is not in the typical situation of computational power operating for only a fraction of total computer usage time. In the typical situation, the arithmetic and logic unit of a less sophisticated computer is idle when a new job is started, when an operating program refers to files, or when additional data inputs are necessary to complete a job.

Time-sharing can be divided into three distinct categories: unrestricted general-purpose, single-program or restricted general-purpose, and dedicated or special-purpose.[27] An unrestricted system is the generally accepted meaning of the unqualified phrase "time-sharing." Such a system provides a user immediate access to the computer and creates the illusion that he is the only user. A single-program or restricted general-purpose time-sharing system closely resembles an unrestricted general-purpose system except that it is a one-language system.[28] Dedicated or special-purpose systems facilitate the execution of specific problems and are generally limited to performing a specialized function. The SAGE air defense system and the American Airline's SABRE system are examples of dedicated systems.

Characteristics of a Multiple-Access-Computer Service Bureau

It should be noted that the users of a time-sharing system may be in the same or in different organizations and they may be located at or some distance from the computer installation. In keeping with the service bureau concept, this study assumes that users represent different organizations, not one of which is located at the computer installation. However, most of the characteristics described are common to any type of a time-sharing system. These characteristics pertain to concepts, hardware, software, servicing capabilities, cost, and control.

Conceptual characteristics. Three separate but complementary concepts characterize a MAC service bureau. These are "on-line," "real-time," and "time-sharing." Time-sharing was described earlier but it is examined again in terms of its relationship to the other two concepts.

The first concept, "on-line," has two applicable meanings. The first meaning applies to earlier data processing systems where the concept served to identify pieces of equipment under the control of the operating program in the computer. With respect to a MAC service bureau, the scope of the concept expands in terms of equipment, geography, and services performed. The equipment used reflects a wide assortment of data origination and communications devices, in addition to the ordinary peripheral machines, all under the control of a special computer program. Furthermore, data origination devices may be located 30 feet or 3,000 miles from the central processor. Distance limitations are dictated primarily by economics and not technology. Services, performed for a number of different entities, are characterized by the elimination of human intervention from the point of input origination and computer processing to the point of information output at various devices. Data can flow over special communications links in one direction only, in one or another direction, or in two directions simultaneously. In effect, on-line systems "increase the burden on the computer so that the efficiency of the man can be increased."[29]

"Real-time" is a measure of responsiveness, implicitly expressed in relative terms. Robert V. Head defines a real-time system as "paralleling data processing with a physical process in such a fashion that the results of the data processing are immediately useful to the physical operation."[30] He adds that "essentially this definition singles out the feedback characteristic of a real-time system as the predominant one by requiring that system results be available in sufficient time to affect the external process."[31] There remains the question of acceptable response time. Is it the almost instantaneous response necessary to control a station in a steel mill from which the computer receives and services randomly received signals from a metering device? Or is a real-time response the receipt and batching of a week's payroll information in time to process employee pay checks and records? Of course, there is no one solution. Head concludes that real-time systems ". . . must satisfy some reasonable criterion of 'immediacy" in providing a response, regardless of whether the input is batched in some way or is in fact processed as soon as received."[32]

The concept of time sharing depends heavily upon the other two concepts described. Each user of a time-sharing system, and each subscriber to such a service in the case of a MAC service bureau, requires a direct link to the central processor. With a number of users, this feature further requires a simultaneous linkage. In addition, an immediate response is necessary, often modified by the type of service demanded. For example, an almost instantaneous response may be necessary for a stock status inquiry while a less stringent response time may be adequate for preparing an invoice. A time-sharing system must be able to sense the priorities implied in this example. Added to a time-sharing system's features of direct, simultaneous, and instantaneous service is the requirement that such a system be:

1. independent to the degree that different services, programs, or devices can be in use separately or in combination during any given period of time.

2. general purpose to the degree that no restriction is placed on the kind of program or application involved[33]

Hardware characteristics. The MAC service bureau differs greatly from a conventional service bureau in the types of hardware employed, especially communications and data storage equipment. For communications purposes, devices are required to originate data, to convert its form, to control its flow, and to insure its integrity. Data origination or terminal devices may have send-only, receive-only, or send-and-receive capabilities. They may take the form of keyboard equipment, meters, punched-card terminals, paper and magnetic tape terminals, or even computers. Data sets convert the electrical signals from these terminal devices into tones for transmission over communication lines. At the MAC service bureau, the tones are interpreted, reconverted into electrical signals, and fed directly to the computer or converted into punched cards, paper or magnetic tape and retained for future processing. Data flow may be controlled by a special computer, the communications multiplexor. Under the control of the central processor, the multiplexor pools the various users, analyzes requests, assembles incoming and outgoing messages, and routes messages through the transmission network. There are capabilities in data sets and in the multiplexor to test messages for completeness, distortion, etc.

Data storage requirements present a challenge to the smooth operation of a MAC service bureau, especially if the users' requirements are file-oriented, as are most business data processing applications. Various levels of storage using magnetic core, drum, disc, tape, and even punched cards are often necessary. Especially important are rapidly accessible random-access-memory units. The interactions between storage levels themselves and the computer are complex. Often, a file multiplexor controlled by the central processor may be used to control traffic to and from and within the data storage units.

Items of equipment such as units which synchronize the operation of a multi-computer installation, common items of peripheral equipment, and machine-prepared logs recording customer use and other information are beyond the scope of this study. Clearly, the operation of a MAC service bureau presents all of the problems inherent in a conventional service bureau in addition to considerations many times more complex.

Software characteristics. Time sharing systems require very elaborate programs. Furthermore, programming is paramount, well ahead of other systems considerations in relative importance. In addition to the application-oriented programs of each user maintained in memory at the MAC service bureau, there are several other types of program. Foremost among these is a program alternatively referred to as an executive, monitor, supervisor, or control. The executive program literally controls the system. The equipment and the other programs operate autonomously only to degrees, never completely. Among the duties of the executive program are establishing a user's priority, allocating and controlling storage, controlling input and output, checking errors, controlling the queue of service requests, etc. Other program types are for general system support. These exist to perform specific functions such as aiding in system development, maintaining files, and off-line processing.[34]

Servicing capabilities and cost characteristics. As of the fall of 1965, there were six commercial time-sharing systems where users could purchase remote, on-line and interactive computer services.[35] These were serving anywhere from 16 to 40 users. Most time-sharing systems are modular in nature. Consequently as demand increases, additional users or subscribers can be added. Keydata Corporation, the nation's first business-oriented MAC service bureau, claims that it can easily expand its existing capacity of more than 200 simultaneous users.[36]

The cost of using a MAC service bureau depends primarily upon the types of services required, processing time, memory storage requirements, terminals used, and communications links provided. Keydata Corporation's subscribers pay about $1,000 per month.[37] The services received by Keydata customers are mainly invoicing and inventory control. A computer manufacturer's division offering scientific, engineering, and business problem-solving services, which are equivalent to having a super desk calculator or a slide rule, charges $350 per month for the following:

1. 25 hours of active on-line connection to the system
2. 2 hours of central processor time
3. 60,000 characters of storage

The division's rate does not include charges for a telephone line, toll calls, and terminal equipment, all of which are provided by local telephone companies. In general, most available time-shared services appear to have an hourly cost of from $5 to $30.[38]

Control characteristics. Of special interest to the CPA are the control characteristics of a particular MAC service bureau's system. With many remote subscribers simultaneously using a common memory, it is important that their respective records and programs be protected. Some systems accomplish this by assuming that the system's programs are debugged and that the users' programs are never debugged.[39] This requires that the system be designed so as to operate in two modes, one when the system's own programs are processing and the other when users' programs are operative. In the latter mode, special hardware sets limits in memory from which users' programs can never leave. At the same time, certain commands which would interfere with the system's operation as a utility and which are reserved for the executive program are prohibited when the computer is operating in a user mode.[40] Glaser and Corbato note that

Within a system in which many user programs are being swapped in and out of memory at a relatively high rate, it is often difficult or impossible, without such protective hardware, to determine the difference between a program that has gone awry and a machine fault.[41]

Keydata Corporation approaches the problem of control in an interesting manner. Console operators are provided preestablished confidential codes or passwords for the various applications. The applications' passwords include the console's identity and a check digit for accuracy. Each operator receives a specified group of passwords only in order to restrict confidential information to a need-to-know basis. For example, the executive payroll can be processed only by persons knowing the appropriate password. Furthermore, a subscriber's files cannot be entered except from his own console. Thus, if another console transmits an appropriate password, the computer senses that the request is not from the correct subscriber's console and denies access to the files.

The importance of control in the Keydata system can be best illustrated by examining a typical invoicing procedure.[42] The console operator enters a customer number and a series of quantity and item numbers. The computer immediately types in the date, invoice number, customer's name and address, item description, unit prices, total item cost, and discounts, and totals the invoice. Stock-out conditions are indicated by a back-order message. All identification numbers include a check digit. The system ascertains the existence of a customer or item number and error messages alert the operator if a customer or item number is non-existent. In addition, three levels of control are used to insure the system's accuracy:

Level One—Dollars billed and units sold for a period of any specified size are accumulated for each subscriber by the system. These are available for inquiry at any time the system is operative. To determine machine accuracy, manual totals may be kept and compared to the system's running totals. The system's running totals can also be used to evaluate the firm's periodic progress.

Level Two—Dollars billed to each customer will be immediately added to a customer's receivables-outstanding field in random-access memory. At the end of the specified time-period, all separate charges made during that period are totalled and compared to the periodic total of dollars billed (described in Level One). In order to detect a situation where an item is correctly invoiced and posted to the proper subscriber's file but to the wrong customer, each customer's balance maintained in disc storage is periodically compared to a magnetic tape upon which the transactions of all subscribers are recorded as they occur. (There are two magnetic tapes. The one described reproduces all inputs into the system. Its primary purpose is record reconstruction. The second tape records actions taken by the computer. Each tape contains the transmitting console's number and a number which establishes the time and date of an entry.) If an error exists, the tape is compared to the disc and the error corrected.

Level Three—At the end of the day, the transaction tape is sorted into transactions-within-user sequence. All dollars billed and units sold by each subscriber are totalled and compared to the system's running totals accumulated for each subscriber as described in Level One. If discrepancies occur, the tape and disc records are compared and the invoice wherein a discrepancy exists is determined. Control totals are automatically reflected in off-line reports.[43]

To protect a subscriber's records from unauthorized alterations, the Keydata system provides two controls.[44] The first, described earlier, is the password. Password restrictions can be placed on certain types of changes such as changing a price list. Secondly, as each change is entered into a system, a magnetic tape records the console's identification number, the operator's initials, the type of change, the old and new information, the time and date of the change, and a sequence number.[45] At month-end, the tape is used to prepare a report of changes by sequenced change number for the subscriber. Operator performance can also be evaluated by reference to the tapes.

MAC Service Bureaus—
Present and Future

Currently, three general types of MAC service bureaus, classified by services rendered, are in various stages of development.[46]

MAC service bureaus offering scientific and engineering problem solving and others providing business-oriented data processing are actively marketing their services. Specialized time-shared information services, similar to American Airline's SABRE System, are also available on a service-bureau basis. The literature indicates that each of these developments portend a phenomenal future for the service-bureau concept.

Present capabilities. Several MAC service bureaus offer scientific and engineering problem-solving services exclusively. Such services are especially attractive for scientists, engineers, and others whose computational requirements "would benefit greatly from the speed and accuracy of a fully automatic, record keeping and computing facility."[47] In effect, the subscribers own a portion of a super calculating machine or slide-rule. The General Electric Company operates more than a dozen such geographically dispersed but communicationally linked installations. Providing for highly responsive man-machine interaction, installations such as these save users' time and increase their effectiveness by allowing them to concentrate on problem solving without first becoming computer technologists. Users originate programs through remotely located keyboard consoles in one of several programming languages available. Generally, users prepare their own programs. Each user compiles, tests, or operates programs developed by him without regard to the activities of other subscribers. Often available are package programs which permit users to debug their own programs with the assistance of the computer. The users' programs can be stored for later use or run immediately through the consoles, which usually have the capability of transmitting and receiving a variety of data. Standard package programs for land survey, analysis of variance, PERT, and many others are often available for the convenience of all subscribers.

A second type of MAC service bureau currently available has the capability of processing the file-oriented requirements of business firms as well as providing computational services. Keydata Corporation's invoicing operations, presented earlier, illustrate the kinds of file-oriented services available. While initially handling billing, inventory, and computational services only, the Keydata system will eventually handle other functions. Shortly, a completely computerized management information system for small- and medium-sized businesses will be available through such organizations.

Through a console, a subscriber can "run the payroll, solve a PERT network, or debug a program just as he would with his own equipment."[48]

Specialized time-shared information systems generally do not permit subscribers to prepare, alter, or modify existing programs from their consoles. Programming services are usually centrally provided. The remote consoles are generally special purpose in design and transmit or receive highly stylized data.[49] Subscribers' records may or may not be maintained by the system and individual subscribers may or may not be permitted to enter data in the system which would alter common files. Examples of specialized MAC service bureaus are stock and bond quotation services and teller services for banks provided by outside organizations. The majority of other such commercially available services are not time-shared systems of the type discussed, but the literature indicates that credit bureaus, economic analysis and forecasting services, construction statistics specialists, and certain industry groups are rapidly moving in that direction.[50]

Future developments. The MAC service bureaus currently in operation are the forerunners of a revolutionary new concept. As local MAC service bureaus and time-shared systems of individual companies, industries, universities, and government grow, they may eventually be interconnected, thus forming a nation-wide network of information utilities.[51] Richard E. Sprague notes that "the term 'information utility' is derived from the public utility which supplies a service to many subscribers for a service charge based on usage."[52] Sprague defines the term as ". . . a service supplied to many subscribers which is, in one way or another, related to information."[53] He concludes that "the service may include the collection, storage, processing, analyzing, computing and display of information. It may go beyond information itself and deal with money or financial commitments or similar functions."[54] One indication that such a concept will in fact evolve is the expectation that time-shared systems will account for nearly half of the $5-billion computer industry sales projected for 1970.[55]

An interesting aspect of the information utility of tomorrow is the potential role of the banking industry as the system's operator. Bankers recognize that improved computers and communications systems offer a solution for eliminating the mountain of negotiable

instruments processed by the industry. Of greater importance however, is the fact that such systems allow the transfer of funds at
electronic speeds within a bank or between banks. For example,
terminal devices connected to a bank's computer and located in retail establishments can automatically transfer funds from a purchaser's account to the retailer's account. Similar devices located
at the purchaser's place of employment can signal the transfer of
funds from the employer's payroll account to the personal accounts
of employees. Situations such as these and many similar ones better
synchronize money flows with the physical flow of goods and services.[56] Money thus becomes even more synonymous with information.

In effect, many types of information are first-order by-products
of money flows. Other types of information can be ultimately traced
to money flows. The emphasis placed by the banking industry upon
improved computers and communications systems and their activity
in providing computerized customer services indicate their awareness of the interaction between money flows and information. Given
the end of such artificially restrictive factors as regulatory laws,
the electronic information processing capabilities and the strategic
financial position of the banking industry may permit it to emerge as
the owner-operator of the information utility system.

The Implications of MAC Service
Bureaus for the Accounting Profession

Although prognostications frequently are proven inaccurate, their
justification rests on the premise that it generally is preferable to
anticipate change rather than to ignore its imminence. The currently existing MAC service bureaus and the future possibility of
a nation-wide system of information utilities will undoubtedly influence accounting practice. It may be useful to examine some of the
implications relating to the areas of theory, auditing, and management services.

Accounting theory. The availability of an instantaneous and
total information processing system, economically attractive to business firms of all sizes and even to individuals, may significantly affect
accounting concepts. As an example, consider the concept of realization. Generally, it considers revenue as realized and thus recorded
in the books at the time of an exchange of goods or services for
liquid assets.[57] The importance of an exchange relates to the con-

cept of objectivity and not to the economic reality of a change in value. Some critics of current practice would eliminate adherence to the realization concept and rely solely upon economic concepts of income.[58] This may be possible if a company manufacturing for inventory has instantaneous external information, unrestricted by geography and other considerations, pertaining to such factors as the current market prices of its product. Internally, the information system can instantaneously provide the status of all goods in process in terms of both factor payments and physical assembly. Assuming that instantaneous information to and from all parts of the economy serves to dampen cyclical fluctuations, quantitative techniques for forecasting future sales volumes, selling prices, and factor costs may be highly reliable. If statistical reliability can be substituted for objectivity, there may be no need for invoking the realization concept in many situations. Thus the recommendations of persons favoring the acceptance of an economic concept of income may become operable.

Auditing. It is submitted that one of the most profound effects of the availability of an instantaneous and total information-processing system will be to bring the role of the auditor and the information systems designer closer together. For departmentalized accounting firms, the audit staff and the management services staff will rely even more heavily upon each other. For smaller CPA firms performing audits, a new breed of local practitioner will emerge: one knowledgeable in accounting, quantitative methods, systems and programming, and data processing. (Because of such stringent requirements upon an individual, one would also expect to see the average size of firms grow larger, or alternatively, the number of small firms decrease.)

The auditor has recently been arming himself with the tools of statistics and probability theory. In addition, many auditors recognize the computer as an aid in auditing and thus have developed computer programming capabilities. These will feel the need for a knowledge of information systems in order that effective controls can be integrated into audit tests without creating inefficiencies in an overall information system.

We should not ignore the services of existing MAC service bureaus for assisting the auditor in devising such audit tests as constructing a sampling table and testing the sample. Placing a terminal in a CPA firm's office can save a material amount of man-hours. A former staff member of a national CPA firm, now employed with a MAC service bureau located in Michigan, illustrated this point with an actual situation. While preparing a statistical sampling table for a client's year-end inventory run, it was suggested that a computer program be designed to perform the testing task once the necessary parameters were established. Through a local service bureau, this was accomplished, turning what had been a better than two man-week task with a desk calculator into a two and one-half day task using a service bureau. (Most of the time was spent for writing the program, which could be used in future years and, with some modification, for other clients.) If a problem-solving type of time-shared system were available, the programming, processing, and testing could have been performed in the CPA firm's office in an estimated one man-day.

Management services. The development of a system of information utilities will allow firms of any size to have computerized management information systems of the type considered in Chapter II. CPA firms with systems capabilities can expect to derive a substantial portion of their billings from systems design and modification engagements. However, in the future, systems design work will require a greater involvement with communications hardware and techniques in addition to an expanded knowledge of computer hardware and software.

Write-up work, tax return preparation, and other similar manually oriented functions currently performed by CPA firms will be completely mechanized. Practicing CPAs of the future will perform advisory and audit services exclusively. Operational, financial, and tax advice will be on a significantly higher plane than generally performed today, if for no other reason than that competition in these areas from banks and management consulting firms will be keen. To be able to perform services of an acceptable caliber, the traditional tools of accountancy must be augmented by mathematics, statistics, operations research, computer technology, and the other resources of an information technologist.

A console located in the CPA's office and connected to the information utility system can serve as an aid in performing management-services work. Simulation techniques applied through the computer can be used to design a client's management-information system. By determining and defining management's objectives, the necessary planning and control functions to accomplish these, and the interaction among a myriad of factors, a quantitative model of an information system can be designed.[59] Values can be assigned to these factors and varied in order that preestablished parameters may be optimized. The console can be used to develop the model or program and to process the simulation. Similarly, the console can be used to assist in developing proposals for clients related to optimal capital structure, inventory policy, capital expenditures budgets, or tax planning.

VII

Summary and Conclusions

Information technology, at an almost revolutionary rate of change, challenges the accounting profession's performance of three functions: reporting financial history, preparing and analyzing decision-making information, and auditing. The practice of performing these functions only through traditional accounting methodology requires re-evaluation in light of this challenge. Disciplines related to accounting such as mathematics, statistics, computer technology, etc., promise a more effective performance of accounting functions when properly integrated with existing methodology. If the accounting profession expands its knowledge boundaries and reaps the benefits available from using the tools of related disciplines effectively, great rewards await. Foremost among these is the knowledge that accounting provides indispensable services for the business community.

From the standpoint of public accounting practice, the management services area requires a very general yet complete knowledge of accounting. Strong capabilities in auditing, taxation, and disciplines related to accounting often are prerequisites for successful entrance into this area. These requirements reflect the relationship between management services and clients' information needs. Information is a precious resource and as such it must receive expert attention. A major portion of such attention should be directed to the management information system. It is here that all areas of accounting and many related disciplines are integrated for the purpose of providing information tailored to the needs of each client.

Often, information truly responsive to clients' needs can be had only with the assistance of a computer. However, firms unable to justify their own computer installation economically but who could benefit from its capabilities need not be denied necessary information. Data-processing service bureaus represent potential components in the management information systems of such firms.

The data-processing service bureau industry, as defined in this study, encompasses a vast assortment of organizations, each displaying distinct characteristics and possessing special skills. Attractive services are available from service bureaus for computerized and non-computerized firms of every description, regardless of factors such as industry classification, data-processing requirements, technical staff composition, geographic dispersion, etc. However, as in purchasing any service, the problem is to select a reputable organization. The industry itself recognizes this and through ADAPSO, the industry trade association, problems related to standards of performance, idea interchange, and image promotion are being resolved. Without a doubt, the future of the industry is impressive, given the efforts of ADAPSO and the continued importance of electronic data processing to all segments of the economy.

The service bureau industry gives the accounting profession an excellent opportunity for a relatively inexpensive and rapid transition from continued exclusive reliance on traditional methodology to a position in the field of information technology. Capital commitments are usually minimal. Special training or knowledge prior to a service bureau relationship is frequently not needed. However, a close working relationship with competent service bureaus often results in the CPA's acquiring new skills and capabilities which supplement his experience with information-processing systems.

The literature is replete with accounts of some CPA firms' successful service-bureau involvements, indicating that some members of the profession recognize the inherent benefits in service-bureau usage. Unfortunately, most articles generally stress one level of service-bureau usage only: that which is the least sophisticated in terms of systems design and information content. Conversely, there is relatively little commentary, in the accounting literature particularly, on the management information systems aspects of service bureau applications. This condition indicates that the accounting profession may be neglecting one of its implied objectives, that of providing information for assisting managerial decision making and control. Given the theoretical and practical limitations of financial accounting, computer-prepared ledgers and statements often provide relatively little useful managerial information.

Adding computer-prepared analytical reports to ledgers and statements while concurrently eliminating manual clerical functions represents a more sophisticated use of service bureaus. Even more sophisticated uses exist for decision-making and control applications in such interdependent areas as procurement, production, and inventory. With advances in communications equipment, computers and peripheral equipment, and software, computerized management information systems employing service bureaus become economically feasible for firms of any size. Herein lies a promising future for the accounting profession. Through the skillful use of facilities such as service bureaus, the practicing accountant can establish himself as an even more vital source of service to his clients. In addition, fees charged for information assistance represent an economically justifiable charge to clients, more so than charges for legislatively-created audit and tax engagements.

The following conditions were found to exist in a sampled population of CPA firms:

1. Relatively few firms were actively involved with service bureaus.
2. A surprisingly small proportion of firms involved with service bureaus employed them at the particular usage level generally referred to in the literature, i.e., automating write-up work.

An inference may be drawn as to the effectiveness of such a commentary on the practices of the majority of accounting firms which could benefit from the automation of their bookkeeping services. In addition, a resistance on the part of practitioners toward new techniques may be indicated. It was further discovered that very few of the accounting firms involved with service bureaus employed them for the more sophisticated uses. However, the following hypotheses generally tended to be substantiated:

1. There are significant differences, statistically defendable, between firms involved and those not involved with service bureaus.

2. There seem to be significant differences between various classes of CPA firms, differentiated according to various types of service bureau involvements.

These differences relate to such factors as size of staff, staff composition, number of clients, billings, management services activity, attitude toward electronic data processing, and others. It is not meant to imply that service bureau usage is solely responsible for any differences. Without a doubt, these differences basically reflect firms' aggressiveness and imagination. Service bureau usage is an effect of these characteristics. In addition, a substantial number of firms, especially those most actively involved with service bureaus, reported that service bureau usage has been a positive factor in terms of a more tolerable work pace, greater productivity, new clients gained, expanded services offered, etc.

Another portion of the study indicated th^t service bureaus and commercial banks of the geographic region in which the CPA firms surveyed are located had unflattering opinions of the CPA as a factor in systems work and of his knowledge and effective use of service bureaus. Their opinions imply the following:

1. Generally, CPA firms appear to be by-passed in the installation and subsequent modification phases of service bureau applications.
2. Frequently, CPA firms seem to ignore possible auditing implications inherent in service bureau applications.
3. Service bureaus and computerized banks offer a broad range of services attractive to CPA firms and to clients of CPA firms.
4. Data-processing services are often marketed by service bureaus and computerized commercial banks through non-computerized banks.

The future effects of the service-bureau industry may be more dramatic than any experienced to date. The continued aggressive entry of commercial banks into the business of offering service bureau-type services presents competition to CPA firms engaged in write-up work. In addition, as the banking industry gains expertise in processing its own more sophisticated data-processing requirements, it is reasonable to assume that services related to these requirements will be offered to the business community. Already, prognostications assert that the banking industry will some day become the purveyor of sophisticated information systems. Of special importance is the challenge banks may provide to many local CPAs acting as part-time controllers for their clients. The expertise of banks in financial matters is unchallenged; and, as they develop systems capabilities, it is reasonable to expect them to provide services resembling, in part at least, the CPA's management services.

A further development in the service bureau concept relates to multiple-access-computer (time-sharing) service bureaus. These organizations are the forerunners of tomorrow's information utilities, a network of integrated service bureaus sharing each other's facilities and providing users with true management information systems without requiring corresponding commitments for equipment or special personnel. Although only a handful of such organizations currently exist, the commentary excited by their accomplishments indicates that they represent a startling new concept in information systems. Moreover, they provide practitioners a versatile new tool for improving their services. If their potential effectiveness is recognized by the profession, the accountant's future is indeed promising.

Appendices

Appendix A

CPA Post Card Questionnaire

Check the category *or categories* that describe your firm (if your firm has more than one office, answer for *your* office *only*.)

Check here

1. Our *office uses* its *own* data processing service bureau, or one in which *our firm* has a financial interest, to service clients

_____

2. Our *office uses* an outside data processing service bureau to service clients.

_____

3. Our office has *clients using* data processing service bureaus *directly*.

_____

4. Our office is *not* in *any* of the *above* categories.

_____

Constantine Konstans
1310 C University Village
East Lansing, Michigan 48823

TO: Managing Partners and Sole Practitioners

In conjunction with The Michigan Association of CPA's study on the use of data processing service bureaus by member firms, please complete the attached post-card and return it to the Association. This study has been undertaken to provide you with knowledge useful in the Computer Age. Your cooperation is vital to the success of this study.

Thank you,

William R. Shaw, President
The Michigan Association of CPAs

Appendix B

CPA Detailed Questionnaire

April 15, 1966

TO: Managing Partners and Sole Practitioners

Thank you for participating in the initial phase of The MACPA's research project on the effect of data processing service bureaus on public practice in Michigan. Approximately 80 percent of the member firms responded. The following is a summary of the results.

Category	Category Description	Responding Firms Number	Percent
1.	Firms using their own service bureau or one in which the firm has a financial interest	9	2
2.	Firms using an outside service bureau	38	9
3.	Firms with clients using service bureaus	120	27
4.	Firms in category 1 and 2	1	
5.	Firms in category 1 and 3	1	
6.	Firms in category 2 and 3	27	6
7.	Firms not in any of the above categories	252	56
		448	100%

Enclosed is a questionnaire representing the study's final phase. While it is formidable in size, there are very few questions which require more than a check mark to register your response. Practitioners pre-testing the questionnaire averaged less than thirty minutes to complete it.

159

Your responses will be completely anonymous. The series of numbers along the right-hand edge of each page of the questionnaire are for the convenience of key punch operators. Your responses will be entered on punch cards and then analyzed with the aid of a CDC 3600 Computer. The results and some useful information on service bureaus and service bureau usage will be made available to you in a booklet at the termination of the study. (Details of the study appeared in the January-February edition of The Michigan CPA.)

A former data processing consultant with a national CPA firm recently commented that CPA firms are not recognizing their opportunity in time to participate effectively in the service bureau industry. To assist you in recognizing and benefiting from that opportunity, the Association has invested time and funds into this study. However, its value to you in this respect will be determined by your assistance. Please return the questionnaire by May 15, 1966.

Thank you again,

William R. Shaw, President

WRS/mg
encs.

INSTRUCTIONS FOR COMPLETING QUESTIONNAIRE

1. Firms having more than one office should complete the questionnaire only for the office to which the questionnaire is addressed.

2. The following are samples of the two main types of questions encountered.

Sample Question 1.

Are you a member of The Michigan Association of CPAs?

Answer Category (Circle ONLY one answer)

Yes	*No*	No, but plan to be	No, and do not plan to be
1	2	3	4

Assuming that you are a member of the Association, you would have circled 1 in response to this question which corresponds, in this question, to a "Yes" response.

Sample Question 2.

If you are a member of The Michigan Association of CPAs,

please indicate by checking in the column provided the reasons for being a member.

Answer Category	*Check here*
a. Feel it is professional responsibility	X
b. Feel it will aid professional development	X
c. Belong *only* because the firm expects it	
d. Other (please specify)_____	

The appropriate reasons for an assumed respondent have been entered. Note that if there was a reason other than one of those specified, space is provided for the respondent to insert, in brief form, the reason(s).

3. *Definitions*

   a. *Business Client*—A proprietorship, partnership, corporation, estate or non-profit institution for whom you perform professional services. Exclude clients for whom only a *personal* 1040 tax return is prepared.

   b. *Management Services*—Engagements *other than* "Write-Up," audit and tax. *Includes* such services as budgets and forecasts; cost system design; work simplification studies; reporting system modification; EDP feasibility studies; cash budgeting, operations research application, etc.

   c. *Systems and Procedures*—Pertains to design or modification of a client's reporting (information) system. It is a facet of Management Services work concerned with procedures, methods and other considerations relevant to the collection, processing and presentation of information.

4. Please place the finished questionnaire into the self-addressed envelope and return to the Association. Make any comments you wish relevant to the study, individual questions, etc., on the back of this page. Thank you.

MACPA STUDY OF THE EFFECTS OF SERVICE BUREAUS ON THE ACCOUNTING PROFESSION

PART I

1. Office classification

    Answer Category (Circle ONLY *one answer)*

Home	Branch	One office firm
1	2	3

    A5

2. Please indicate the size of the largest city within 20 miles of your office or size of city in which your office is located, whichever is larger.

    Answer Category (Circle ONLY *one answer)*

Under 1,000	1,000- 5,000	5,001- 10,000	10,001- 20,000	20,001- 40,000	40,001- 80,000	80,001- 120,000	120,001- 200,000	Over 200,000
1	2	3	4	5	6	7	8	9

    6

3. Please indicate the total *number* of business clients (see definition on instructions page) served in calendar year 1965.

    Answer Category (Circle ONLY *one answer)*

10% or Under	11- 30	31- 50	51- 100	101- 150	151- 200	201- 250	251- 300	Over 300
1	2	3	4	5	6	7	8	9

    7

4. Please estimate your gross billings for 1965.

    Answer Category (Circle ONLY *one answer)*

Less than 12,000	12,000- 24,999	25,000- 49,999	50,000- 99,999	100,000- 250,000	Over 250,000
1	2	3	4	5	6

    8

5. Please estimate the percent of gross billings derived from Management Services (see definition on instructions page) engagements in 1965.

    Answer Category (Circle ONLY *one answer)*

None	5% or Under	6- 10%	11- 15%	16- 20%	21- 25%	26- 30%	31- 35%	Over 35%
1	2	3	4	5	6	7	8	9

    9

SPECIAL INSTRUCTIONS FOR QUESTION 6:

Answer the following question *only* if the answer to question 5 was *other than* "none."

6. For the past few years, have billings from Management Services engagements *increased* at a *relatively faster rate* than billings from all other services combined?

Answer Category (Circle ONLY one answer)

Yes	No, Slower	No, about the same	
1	2	3	10

7. Professional Personnel Characteristics—*include* partners but *exclude* clerical and administrative help. Insert the appropriate figures in the right hand column of the table provided.

Answer Category	*Answer in this column*	
a. Number with primary training in accounting	_____	11
b. Number with primary training other than in accounting	_____	14
c. Total staff (a + b)	_____	17
d. Number of CPAs	_____	20
e. Number of college graduates	_____	22
f. Number of staff in a separate Management Services section	_____	25
g. Number of staff who spend over 50% of their time on Management Services work	_____	27
h. Number of staff with over 80 hours in formal EDP training	_____	29
i. Number of staff performing systems and procedures work (see definition on instructions page)	_____	31

8. Characteristics of Business Clients—Please *estimate* the *percent* of the total *number* of business clients in each of the following categories.

Answer Category	*%of bus. clients*	
a. Clients for whom journals and ledgers are prepared and posted in addition to preparing monthly or quarterly statements	_____	33
b. Clients for whom you prepare monthly or quarterly statements *but* who journalize and post their *own* transactions	_____	35
c. Clients who prepare their *own* financial statements	_____	37
TOTAL BUSINESS CLIENTS (a + b + c = 100%)	100%	
d. Percent of business clients using their own or leased computer and/or tab equipment	_____	39

9. In 1965, approximately how many business clients or potential clients requested such EDP services as feasibility studies, computer selection, and EDP facility expansion or reduction?

Answer Category *(Circle* ONLY *one answer)*

None	1	2	3	4-5	6-7	8-9	10-15	Over 15	
1	2	3	4	5	6	7	8	9	41

SPECIAL INSTRUCTIONS FOR QUESTION 10:

Answer the following question *only* if the answer to question 9 was *other than* "none."

10. If the answer to question 9 was *other than* "none," indicate in terms of frequency your disposition of the request. (The *most* frequent disposition will be marked "1," the *next* most frequent "2," etc.)

	Answer Category		*Ranking*	
a.	Our firm performed the service alone		_____	42
b.	We received assistance from another CPA firm		_____	43
c.	We received assistance from a computer manufacturer's representative		_____	44
d.	Client turned to an outside non-CPA consultant		_____	45
e.	Other (please specify)_____			
	_____		_____	46

11. Compared to the effect EDP has had to date on the practice of public accounting, what do you believe will be the effect in five years?

Answer Category *(Circle* ONLY *one answer)*

Much greater	Greater	About the same	Less	Much less	None	
1	2	3	4	5	6	47

12. Do you feel that other CPA firms with which you are acquainted are well informed on the services data processing service bureaus offer?

Answer Category *(Circle* ONLY *one answer)*

Yes	Not Sure	No	
1	2	3	48

13. Is your office, or one in which your firm has a financial interest, currently using its own electronic computer or tabulating equipment to service business clients?

Answer Category (Circle ONLY one answer)

No	No, but computer on order	No, but tab equip. on order	Yes, computer	Yes, tab equip.	Yes, combin. of 4 and 5	
1	2	3	4	5	6	49

14 Does your office use an outside service bureau to service business clients or do *some* of your clients use a service bureau directly?

Answer Category (Circle ONLY one answer)

No	Office uses	Clients use	Combination of 2 and 3	
1	2	3	4	50

15. From which source(s) did your office acquire its knowledge of service bureaus? (Place a check mark next to the appropriate category or categories in the column provided.)

Answer Category	Check here	
a. Discussion with a CPA using service bureaus	_____	51
b. Staff member formerly with a service bureau	_____	52
c. Service bureau representative	_____	53
d. Computer manufacturer's representative	_____	55
e. EDP trade magazine	_____	54
f. Accounting literature	_____	56
g. MACPA educational program or literature	_____	57
h. Other (please specify)_____	_____	58

16. Which of the following answer categories are reasons why, in your opinion, some CPA firms have not acquired a knowledge of service bureaus?

Answer Category	Check here	
a. Insufficient professional literature on the subject	_____	59
b. Lack of service bureau selling effort	_____	60
c. Have no clients that could benefit from EDP	_____	61
d. Fear too many EDP-accounting problems	_____	62
e. Not interested	_____	63
f. Other (please specify)_____	_____	64

17. Does your office believe that service bureau applications will tend to reduce gross billings?

Answer Category (Circle ONLY *one answer)*

Yes	No	Not sure	
1	2	3	65

SPECIAL INSTRUCTIONS FOR QUESTION 18:

Answer the following question *only* if your office does *not* use service bureaus to service business clients and/or does *not* recommend service bureau usage to business clients for their direct usage.

18. If your office does *not* use service bureaus to service business clients and/or does *not* recommend service bureaus to business clients for their direct use, what are your reasons?

	Answer Category	Check here	
a.	Service bureaus have received poor publicity	_____	66
b.	Poor past experiences with recommendations	_____	67
c.	Communication difficult with service bureaus	_____	68
d.	Not familiar with their capabilities and limitations	_____	69
e.	Fear loss of data control	_____	70
f.	Feel that results not worth the effort	_____	71
g.	Have no clients that could benefit from service bureaus	_____	72
h.	They are incompetent to render services	_____	73
i.	It is unethical	_____	74
j.	Fear loss of clients	_____	75
k.	Other (please specify)_____	_____	B5

19. Does your staff know of any service bureaus located within 20 miles of your office?

Answer Category (Circle ONLY *one answer)*

Yes	Not sure	No	
1	2	3	6

20. Please indicate which *category or categories* best describe your office.

	Answer Category	Check here	
a.	Our office *no longer uses* its *own* electronic computer or tab equipment in servicing clients	_____	7

    b. Our office *no longer uses* an *outside* service
       bureau(s) in servicing clients   _____   8
    c. Our firm is *not* in *any* of the *above* categories   _____   9

SPECIAL INSTRUCTIONS FOR QUESTION 21:
Answer the following question *only* if you checked category a, and/
or b in question 20.

21. Please state briefly your reason(s) for your answer in question 20._____

_____

_____

_____

_____

22A. Have you lost engagements or business clients to a service bureau?

Answer Category (Circle ONLY *one answer)*

Yes, engagements	*Yes, clients*	*Combination of 1 and 2*	*No*	
1	2	3	4	10

22B. If yes, please indicate the type(s) of service bureau(s) involved.

Answer Category	*Check here*	
1. Bank	_____	11
2. CPA-owned	_____	12
3. Independent	_____	13
4. Computer manufacturer-owned	_____	14
5. Other (please specify)_____	_____	15

22C. Please indicate the type(s) of engagement(s) involved.

Answer Category	*Check here*	
1. Journalize and post transactions and prepare financial statements	_____	16
2. Prepare financial statements	_____	17
3. Tax returns	_____	18
4. Management services	_____	19
5. Systems and procedures	_____	20
6. Other (please specify)_____	_____	21

22D. Please indicate the *number* of engagements or business clients lost, whichever is larger.

Answer Category (Circle ONLY one answer)

1	2	3	4	5	6-10	11-15	16-20	Over 20	
1	2	3	4	5	6	7	8	9	22

PART II

23A. Please estimate the *percent* of the total number of business clients serviced by your office through the use of an outside service bureau or one in which the firm has a financial interest.

Answer Category (Circle ONLY one answer)

5% or Under	6-10	11-15	16-20	21-25	26-30	31-40	41-50	Over 50%	
1	2	3	4	5	6	7	8	9	B23

23B. Approximately what *percent* of your gross billings does this represent?

Answer Category (Circle ONLY one answer)

5% or Under	6-10	11-15	16-20	21-25	26-30	31-40	41-50	Over 50%	
1	2	3	4	5	6	7	8	9	24

24. What factors influenced your office's decision to use a service bureau in order to service business clients?

Answer Category — Check here

a. Good experience of other CPAs using service bureaus _____ 25

b. Sold on the idea by a service bureau representative _____ 26

c. Needed to increase the productivity of practice _____ 27

d. Client inquired after seeing another's service bureau output _____ 28

e. Articles in accounting periodicals _____ 29

f. MACPA training program or literature _____ 30

g. Other (please specify)_____ _____ 31

25A. Type of service bureau most frequently used *or* most important in terms of client billings derived from its use.

Answer Category (Circle ONLY *one answer)*

Equip. Mfgr. Sub.	Inde- pendent	Bank	Our own	Another CPAs	CPA computer Co-op	A client's idle machine time	Other	
1	2	3	4	5	6	7	8	32

25B. Type of equipment utilized by the service bureau referred to in question 25A.

Answer Category (Circle ONLY *one answer)*

Tab	Stored program computer	Combination of 1 and 2	
1	2	3	33

25C. Type of program generally utilized by that service bureau for servicing your needs.

Answer Category (Circle ONLY *one answer)*

Package	Package with modifications when needed	Custom	
1	2	3	34

25D. Miles distance between your office and that service bureau.

Answer Category (Circle ONLY *one answer)*

10 miles or Under	11- 20	21- 30	31- 50	51- 100	101- 300	301- 500	501- 800	Over 800m	
1	2	3	4	5	6	7	8	9	35

25E. Does that service bureau offer formal training or orientation programs to familiarize users with its capabilities and limitations?

Answer Category (Circle ONLY *one answer)*

Yes	No	
1	2	36

25F. Does that service bureau adequately train or familiarize your office with the particular jobs it is processing for you?

Answer Category (Circle ONLY *one answer)*

Yes	No	
1	2	37

SPECIAL INSTRUCTIONS FOR QUESTION 26:

Answer the following question *only* if your office uses more than one service bureau.

26. If your office uses more than one service bureau, what are your reasons?

Answer Category
Check here

   a. Prior practice of using only one service bureau proved risky because service bureau went out of business   _____ 38

   b. Feel one source of service risky   _____ 39

   c. Gives us more flexibility in servicing clients because of differing service bureau capabilities   _____ 40

   d. Currently phasing over to one service bureau   _____ 41

   e. Other (please specify)_____   _____ 42

27. What are some of the problems your office encountered in using a service bureau to service clients?

Answer Category
Check here

   a. Time delays and scheduling problems   _____ 43

   b. Poor CPA-service bureau communication   _____ 44

   c. Clients' chart of accounts altered   _____ 45

   d. Clients' reports altered   _____ 46

   e. Clients' fear of loss of business documents   _____ 47

   f. Service bureau attempts to replace CPA in systems and procedures work   _____ 48

   g. Other (please specify)_____   _____ 49

28. What services do you receive from the service bureau(s) you currently utilize?

Answer Category
Check here

   a. General ledger and financial statements   _____ 50

   b. Tax returns   _____ 51

   c. Payroll   _____ 52

   d. Labor distribution   _____ 53

   e. Receivables aging   _____ 54

   f. Payables distribution   _____ 55

g. Sales analysis _____ 56
h. Control application, i.e. production, inventory, etc. _____ 57
i. Year-end inventory run _____ 58
j. Billing _____ 59
k. Other (please specify)_____ _____ 60

---

29. For which type of service has the service bureau generally proved *most* effective?

Answer Category (Circle ONLY one answer)

Results similar for all applications	General ledger and financial statements	Tax returns	Labor dist. and payroll	Payables Dist.
1	2	3	4	5

Billings and receivables aging	Some control function	Some analysis	Year-end inventory run	
6	7	8	9	61

30. Generally, who prepares the clients' business documents into machine-readable form?

Answer Category (Circle ONLY one answer)

CPA firm	Client	Service bureau	Other source	Combination of 1 and 2
1	2	3	4	5

Combination of 1 and 3	Combination of 2 and 3	Some other combination	
6	7	8	62

31. Generally, in what form is data sent to the service bureau?

Answer Category (Circle ONLY one answer)

Source documents	Some combo of 3 thru 8	Punched Cards	Microfilm	Punched paper tape
1	2	3	4	5

Dataphone	Optical font tape	Worksheet listings	Other	
6	7	8	9	63

32. Has using your own or an outside service bureau affected any of the following?

Answer Category | Check here
| a. Professional staff increased | _____ | 64 |
| b. Professional staff decreased | _____ | 65 |

c. Non-professional staff increased   _____   66
d. Non-professional staff decreased   _____   67
e. Staff trained in EDP   _____   68
f. Have added persons with EDP experience   _____   69
g. Are seeking people with EDP experience   _____   70
h. Reduced need for traditionally trained accountants   _____   71
i. Have a different mix of engagements   _____   72
j. Number of business clients have increased   _____   73
k. Fee structure higher   _____   74
l. Fee structure lower   _____   75
m. Staff (pro and non-pro) total compensation higher   _____   C5
n. Staff (pro and non-pro) total compensation lower   _____   6
o. Have more time for staff development program   _____   7
p. Work pace less hectic   _____   8
q. Other (please specify)_____   _____   9

33. What provisions does your office make to ascertain the integrity of the service bureau's processing?

Answer Category (Circle ONLY *one answer)*

Question never arose	Using own installation	Require info. on in-house controls	Examine the processing procedure
1	2	3	4

Examine program	Examine processing procedure and program	Obtaining flow charts and description of processing to include program	
5	6	7	10

34. What provisions does your office make to assure the integrity of data moving between your office and a service bureau regardless of the medium of transfer; i.e. messenger, mail, dataphone, etc.?

Answer Category (Circle ONLY *one answer)*

None necessary	Question never arose	Require info. on transfer system	Test the transfer system	Use our own installation	
1	2	3	4	5	11

34A. For approximately how many years has your firm used an outside service bureau and/or your own service bureau to service clients?

Answer Category (Circle ONLY one answer)

1 yr.	*2 yrs.*	*3 yrs.*	*4 yrs.*	*5 yrs.*	*6 yrs.*	*7 yrs.*	*8 yrs.*	*Over 8 yrs.*	
1	2	3	4	5	6	7	8	9	12

(If question numbering is not consecutive, omission of questions 23 through 34 is intentional)

PART III

35A. Please estimate the *percent* of the total number of business clients directly utilizing the facilities of a service bureau.

Answer Category (Circle ONLY one answer)

5% or Under	*6-10*	*11-15*	*16-20*	*21-25*	*26-30*	*31-35*	*36-40*	*Over 40%*	
1	2	3	4	5	6	7	8	9	C 13

35B. Approximately what *percent* of your *gross billings* does this represent?

5% or Under	*6-10*	*11-15*	*16-20*	*21-25*	*26-30*	*31-40*	*41-50*	*Over 50%*	
1	2	3	4	5	6	7	8	9	14

36 What factors prompted your clients to use a service bureau?

Answer Category	*Check here*	
a. Clients' staff suggested	_____	15
b. Service bureau contacted clients	_____	16
c. Recommended by our firm	_____	17
d. Recommended by an outside consultant	_____	18
e. Recommended by clients' business acquaintances	_____	19
f. Recommended by clients' trade association	_____	20
g. Other (please specify)_____	_____	21

37. Did utilizing a service bureau cause initial and subsequent systems and procedures modifications for *any* clients?

Answer Category (Circle ONLY one answer)

Yes	*No*	*Not Sure*	
1	2	3	22

SPECIAL INSTRUCTIONS FOR QUESTION 38:

Answer the following question *only* if your answer to question 37 was "*Yes*."

38. If the answer to the previous question was "Yes," who performed the systems and procedures work for these clients?

	Answer Category	Check here	
a.	Our office did for almost all of the cases	_____	23
b.	Our office did for approximately 50% of the cases	_____	24
c.	Our office did for less than 50% of the cases	_____	25
d.	Clients' staff	_____	26
e.	Service bureau	_____	27
f.	Outside consultant	_____	28
g.	Another CPA firm	_____	29
h.	Other (please specify)_____	_____	30

SPECIAL INSTRUCTIONS FOR QUESTION 39:

Answer the following question *only* if *your* office *recommends* the use of *specific* service bureaus to clients.

39. If your office recommends the use of *specific* service bureaus to clients, what are the reasons?

	Answer Category	Check here	
a.	Good in-house processing and control	_____	31
b.	Communicates and cooperates well with our firm	_____	32
c.	Timely service	_____	33
d.	Reasonable fee structure	_____	34
e.	Actual fees in line with quoted fees	_____	35
f.	Excellent systems and programming help	_____	36
g.	Equipment adequate to service our clients' needs	_____	37
h.	Consults with us on client systems and procedure changes	_____	38
i.	Other (please specify)_____	_____	39

40. For the present and for one year ago, *rank* the different types of service bureaus from 1 thru 5 in terms of the *number* of clients using a particular type. (Please mark the type *most* clients are using with the number "1.")

	Rank in descending order of usage	
Service Bureau Types	*Present*	*Year ago*
a. Bank	_____	41
b. Other CPA's installation	_____	43
c. Equipment manufacturer's subsidiary	_____	45
d. Independent or division	_____	49
e. Other (please specify _____	_____	47

41. Indicate the reasons why in question 40, the service bureau in first place under the "Present" column is so ranked.

	Check here
Answer Category	
a. Proximity to client	_____ 50
b. Service bureau selling effort	_____ 51
c. Reflects timely processing service	_____ 52
d. Reflects competitive fee structure	_____ 53
e. Reflects systems and procedures capabilities	_____ 54
f. Reflects programming capabilities	_____ 55
g. Reflects ability to communicate accounting-wise	_____ 56
h. Reflects extra services at little or no cost	_____ 57
i. Reflects availability of capital for equipment and personnel	_____ 58
j. Other (please specify)_____	_____ 59

SPECIAL INSTRUCTIONS FOR QUESTION 42:

Answer the following question *only* if *some* of your clients use more than one service bureau.

42. If some clients use more than one service bureau, what are their reasons?

	Answer Category	Check here	
a.	Don't know	_____	60
b.	Price considerations	_____	61
c.	Expand variety of services available	_____	62
d.	Maintain flexibility by having other service source	_____	63
e.	Recommended by our firm	_____	64
f.	Other (please specify)_____	_____	65

43. What types of services are clients obtaining from service bureaus?

	Answer Category	Check here	
a.	Clients' personnel use service bureau equipment	_____	66
b.	Programming assistance	_____	67
c.	Systems and procedures assistance	_____	68
d.	Billings	_____	69
e.	Various analyses	_____	70
f.	Control applications, i.e. production, inventory, etc.	_____	71
g.	Using as a transition to their own EDP installation	_____	72
h.	Financial statements and general ledger processing	_____	73
i.	Payroll	_____	74
j.	Back-up and peak-load assistance for clients' EDP installation	_____	75
k.	Scientific applications	_____	D5
l.	Other (please specify)_____	_____	6

44. What types of equipment do the *majority* of service bureaus used by your clients utilize?

Answer Category (Circle ONLY *one answer)*

Tab	Stored-program computer	Combination of 1 and 2	Don't know	
1	2	3	4	7

45. With what types of programs are the *majority* of your clients using service bureaus having *most* of their work processed?

Answer Category (Circle ONLY one answer)

Package	Custom	Don't know	
1	2	3	8

46. What provisions does your office make to ascertain the integrity of a service bureau's processing?

Answer Category (Circle ONLY one answer)

Question never arose	Using own installation	Require info. on in-house controls	Examine the processing procedure
1	2	3	4

Examine processing procedure and program	Examine programs	Obtain flow charts and description of processing to include program	
5	6	7	9

47. What provisions does your office make to assure the integrity of data moving between your client and a service bureau regardless of the medium of transfer, i.e. messenger, mail, dataphone, etc.?

Answer Category (Circle ONLY one answer)

None necessary	Question never arose	Require info. on transfer system	Test the transfer system	Use our own installation	
1	2	3	4	5	10

48. For opinion audit clients starting to use service bureaus, are there generally any substantial changes in the audit program?

Answer Category (Circle ONLY one answer)

Yes	No	No, but there are some minor changes	No clients in this category	
1	2	3	4	11

49. What effect did client usage of service bureaus have on your firm?

	Answer Category	Check here	
a.	None	_____	12
b.	Enabled us to expand our services to clients	_____	13
c.	Created a demand for more proficient staff	_____	14
d.	Was a factor in our increased gross billings	_____	15
e.	Enabled us to acquire more clients because of increased proficiency in EDP matters	_____	16
f.	Other (please specify)_____	_____	17

50.   For approximately how many years have your clients been using
      service bureaus?

Answer Category (*Circle* ONLY *one answer*)

1 yr.	2 yrs.	3 yrs.	4 yrs.	5 yrs.	6 yrs.	7 yrs.	8 yrs.	Over 8 yrs.	
1	2	3	4	5	6	7	8	9	18

Appendix C

Service Bureau-Commercial
Bank Questionnaire

March 17, 1966

Dear Sir:

The Michigan Association of Certified Public Accountants is currently undertaking a research project to determine the effects electronic data processing is having on the accounting profession in Michigan. In conjunction therewith, we would appreciate your cooperation in completing the enclosed questionnaire only if your bank offers data processing services for customers of the type clients of CPAs or CPAs themselves would find attractive.

The questions are all objective in nature, requiring that you circle an appropriate number corresponding to your intended response or that you check certain applicable categories. Your response will be *completely anonymous* and the questionnaire requires less than ten minutes to complete.

Please help us in helping our members recognize the potential benefits inherent in their direct use and in their clients' use of your services. We are preparing a directory of banks offering these service for our members; therefore you may sign the questionnaire or you may write to us under separate cover if you wish to be included on this list along with a brief description of your services. Please use the envelope enclosed for your convenience in returning the questionnaire to us. Thank you.

Very truly yours,
William R. Shaw
President

WRS/nm
encs.

March 17, 1966

Dear Sir:

The Michigan Association of Centified Public Accountants is currently undertaking a research project in order to determine the effects electronic data processing is having on the accounting profession in Michigan. In conjunction therewith, we would appreciate your cooperation in completing the enclosed questionnaire only if you offer commercial, as opposed to scientific, data processing services. The questions are all objective in nature, requiring only that you circle an appropriate number corresponding to your intended response or that you check certain applicable categories. Trial runs undertaken by a group of your Associates averaged less than ten minutes for completing this questionnaire. Your response will be *completely anonymous.*

Please help us in helping our members recognize the potential benefits inherent in their direct use and in their clients' use of your services. We are preparing a directory of service bureaus offering these services for our members; therefore you may sign the questionnaire or you may write to us under separate cover if you wish to be included on this list along with a brief description of your services.

The Computer Age is upon us and only through cooperation will we all benefit. A return envelope is enclosed for your convenience in returning the questionnaire to us. Thank your.

Very truly yours,
William R. Shaw
President

WRS/nm
encs.

THE MICHIGAN ASSOCIATION OF CERTIFIED PUBLIC ACCOUNTANTS DATA PROCESSING SERVICES STUDY

NOTE: If you are a multi-branch operation, answer only for your branch.

1. Do you operate a *stored-program* computer or tabulating equipment which you either *own* or *lease?*

Answer Category (Circle ONLY one answer)

Yes, stored-program computer	Yes, tab	Combination of 1 and 2	No
1	2	3	4

2. How many customers did you serve in 1965?

Answer Category (Circle ONLY one answer)

Under 10	10-25	26-50	51-100	101-200	201-300	301-400	401-500	Over 500
1	2	3	4	5	6	7	8	9

3. What *percent* of the number of customers were direct CPA users?

Answer Category (Circle ONLY one answer)

None	5% or Under	6-10	11-15	16-20	21-25	26-30	31-40	Over 40%
1	2	3	4	5	6	7	8	9

4. What *percent* of the number of customers were referred by CPAs?

Answer Category (Circle ONLY one answer)

None	Under 5% or	6-10	11-15	16-20	21-25	26-30	31-40	Over 40%
1	2	3	4	5	6	7	8	9

5. Do you feel that the majority of CPAs in your marketing area are adequately apprised of and know how to use the services you offer?

Answer Category (Circle ONLY one answer)

Yes, very much so	Yes, fairly so	No	Don't know	Apprised of services but don't know how to use
1	2	3	4	5

6. For customers who are also clients of CPAs, who performs *most* of the systems work, in terms of the number of applications, associated with setting up an application?

We do	CPAs do	Divided almost evenly between us and CPAs	Sources other than us or CPAs
1	2	3	4

Answer Category (Circle ONLY one answer)

7. How proficient are the majority of CPAs you deal with in respect to installing systems?

Answer Category (Circle ONLY one answer)

Very proficient	Good	Fair	Poor	Very poor	Don't know	They don't perform systems work
1	2	3	4	5	6	7

8. Does your firm follow the practice of consulting with a customer's CPA firm for first-time applications, or modifications of existing ones?

Answer Category (Circle ONLY one answer)

Always	Usually	Sometimes	Rarely	Never
1	2	3	4	5

9. Do *first-time* CPA users of your services, or CPAs whose audit clients use your services for the *first time,* approach you about the controls in your processing prior to such use?

Answer Category (Circle ONLY one answer)

All do	Most do	Some do	Very few do	Question never arose
1	2	3	4	5

10. Do you offer formal training or informal assistance for CPA users or for CPAs whose clients use your services?

Answer Category (Circle ONLY one answer)

Yes, formal training	Yes, informal assistance	Combination of 1 and 2	No
1	2	3	4

11. Which of the following services do you offer? (Please check those offered.)

Answer Category   Check here

a. Equipment usage by customers' personnel   _____

b. Programming assistance   _____

c. Custom systems design and installation   _____

d. General ledger and financial statements   _____

e. Tax returns   _____

f. Payroll   _____

g. Various analyses such as sales and receivables aging   _____

h. Various control applications such as production and inventory control   _____

i. Billing   _____

j. Operations research applications such as PERT   _____

k. Scientific applications   _____

l. Other (please indicate)_____

_____

12. Do you also offer customer services of the type indicated in question 11 to banks which do *not* maintain their *own* data processing installation *but* who in turn offer these services to *their* customers?

Answer Category (Circle ONLY one answer)

Yes	*No*
1	2

THANK YOU FOR YOUR ASSISTANCE—ADD ANY COMMENTS YOU WISH ON THE BACK OF THIS QUESTIONNAIRE.

Appendix D[1]

Statistical Measures Employed

The Kolmogorov-Smirnov two-sample test is sensitive to many differences in distributions from which samples are drawn.[2] In particular, it may be used to test the null hypothesis that the distributions do not differ against the alternative that one distribution is stochastically larger, i.e. that more observations fall in the lower categories of one distribution than of the other. Although the Kolmogorov-Smirnov test assumes continuously distributed random variables, failure to meet this assumption results in a conservative test.[3] For large samples ($N_1 > 40$, $N_2 > 40$), the test statistic is a function of the maximum differences, D, (in the hypothesized direction) between the cumulative sample distributions. This function of D is distributed as Chi-square with two degrees of freedom. Values of D sufficient for rejection of the null hypothesis are given below for three probabilities of type I error (erroneous rejection of the null hypothesis).

Marginals	P < .001	P < .01	P < .05
60.61	.34	.28	.23
61.62	.34	.28	.23

1. These measures of significance merely indicate that the inferences drawn from the survey data can be accepted as meaningful and statistically supportable.

2. Sidney Siegel, *Nonparametric Statistics: for the Behavioral Sciences* (New York: McGraw-Hill Book Company, Inc., 1956), pp. 127-36.

3. L. A. Goodman, "Kolmogorov-Smirnov Tests for Psychological Research," *Psychological Bulletin* (March, 1954), pp. 160-68.

Bibliography

Books

Accounting Terminology Bulletin No. 1. New York: American Institute of Certified Public Accountants, 1953.

Allen, John W., *et al. Marketing Your Bank Computer Services Profitably.* Boston: Warren Gorham and Lamont, Inc., 1965.

Barnhart, Clarence L. (ed.). *The American College Dictionary.* New York: Harper and Brothers Publishers, 1951.

Becker, Joseph and Robert M. Hayes. *Information Storage and Retrieval: Tools, Elements, Theories.* New York: John Wiley and Sons, Inc., 1963.

Bierman, Harold, Jr. *Financial and Managerial Accounting: An Introduction.* New York: The Macmillan Company, 1963.

Boutell, Wayne S. *Auditing With the Computer.* Los Angeles: University of California Press, 1965.

Carey, John L. *The Concept of Management Services by CPAs.* New York: American Institute of Certified Public Accountants, 1959.

_____. *The CPA Plans for the Future.* New York: American Institute of Certified Public Accountants, 1965.

Chapin, Ned. *An Introduction to Automatic Computers.* 2d ed. Princeton, New Jersey: D. Van Nostrand Company, Inc., 1963.

Computer Research Study No. 1. New York: American Institute of Certified Public Accountants, 1966.

Computer Research Study No. 3: Computer Applications to Accounting Operations. New York: The American Institute of Certified Public

Directory of Bank Automation. Park Ridge, Illinois: NABAC, The Association for Bank Audit, Control and Operation, 1966.
Accountants, 1966.

Edwards, Edgar O. and Philip W. Bell. *The Theory and Measurement of Business Income.* Los Angeles: University of California Press, 1964.

187

Electronic Data Processing: V—The Use of Computer Service Bureaux. London, England: The Association of Certified and Corporate Accountants, 1964.

Elliott, C. Orville and Robert S. Wasley. *Business Information Processing Systems.* Homewood, Illinois: Richard D. Irwin, Inc., 1965.

Gallagher, James D. *Management Information Systems and the Computer.* New York: American Management Association, 1961.

Gregory, Robert H. and Richard L. Van Horn. *Automatic Data Processing Systems: Principles and Procedures.* 2nd ed. Belmont, California: Wadsworth Publishing Company, Inc., 1963.

Haga, Enoch. *Understanding Automation.* Elmhurst, Illinois: The Business Press, 1965.

Head, Robert V. *Real-Time Business Systems.* Holt, Rinehart, Winston, Inc., 1964.

Kaufman, Felix. *Electronic Data Processing and Auditing.* New York: The Ronald Press Company, 1961.

Management of an Accounting Practice: MAP 18. New York: American Institute of Certified Public Accountants, 1963.

Martin, E. Wainwright, Jr. *Electronic Data Processing: An Introduction.* Revised ed. Homewood, Illinois: Richard D. Irwin, Inc., 1965.

McRae, F. W. *The Impact of Computers on Accounting.* London, England: John Wiley and Sons, Ltd., 1965.

Neuschel, Richard F. *Management by System.* New York: McGraw-Hill Book Company, Inc., 1960.

Palmer, Leonard J. *Service Center Organization and Control.* Detroit: Burroughs Corporation, 1964.

Seigel, Sidney. *Nonparametric Statistics: For the Behavioral Sciences.* New York: McGraw-Hill Book Company, Inc., 1956.

Articles and Periodicals

Abbott, Charles. "Buy, Lease, Share a Computer—Or Utilize a Service Bureau?" *Computers and Automation,* IX, 2 (February, 1960), 15-18.

Adams, Charles W. "Man-Machine Collaboration," in *Data Processing Yearbook* (Detroit: American Data Processing, Inc., 1965), 75-80.

"Automatic Data Processing—Services by Suppliers of Equipment," *Dun's Review and Modern Industry,* LXXXVII, 1, Part 2 (January, 1966), 131-32.

Axelson, K. S. "The Development of Management Services in the Public Accounting Firms," *Management Controls,* X, 1 (New York: Peat, Marwick, Mitchell and Co., January, 1963), 3-7.

Bagshaw, A. R. "Organization of a Computing Service for Industry and Commerce," *The Computer Journal,* IV, 2 (July, 1961), 181-83.

"Banks Open a New Window," *Business Week*, No. 1833 (October 17, 1964), 156, 158, 160, 163.

Basson, M. B. "Expanded Bank Services Through Automation: Opportunity or Trap?," in *Proceedings of the 1964 National Automation Conference* (New York: The American Bankers Association, 1964), 247-51.

Bates, W. J. "Business Systems in Transition," *Data Processing for Management*, V, 3 (March, 1963), 19-23.

Bauer, Walter F. "On-Line Systems—Their Characteristics and Motivations," Reprint from *On-Line Computing Systems*. Detroit: American Data Processing, Inc., 1965.

Beyer, Robert. "Management Services—Time for Decision," *The Journal of Accountancy*, CXIX, 3 (March, 1965), 43-52.

Blumberg, Donald F. "Role of the Service Bureau in Information Processing," in *Proceedings of the October 15, 1962, Management Symposium* (Abington, Pennsylvania: Association of Data Processing Service Organizations, 1962), 5-12.

——————. "Time Sharing: Some Comments and Predictions," *Data Processing Magazine*, VII, 9 (September, 1965), 44-45, 50.

Boutell, Wayne S. "Business Oriented Computers: A Frame of Reference," *The Accounting Review*, XXXIX, 2 (April, 1964), 305-11.

Boyle, Edwin T. "What the Computer Means to the Accounting Profession," *The Journal of Accountancy*, CXXI, 1 (January, 1956), 56-67.

"By-Laws of the Association of Data Processing Service Organizations, Inc." in *Proceedings of the October 28 and 29, 1963, Management Symposium* (Abington, Pennsylvania: Association of Data Processing Service Organizations, 1963), 11.

Camenish, Walter. Comments in the *Proceedings of the January 20, 1961, ADAPSO Management Symposium* (Abington, Pennsylvania: Association of Data Processing Service Organizations, 1961), 18.

Carey, John L. "The Impact of Computers on Practice," *The CPA*, XLV, 3 (March, 1965), 3-4.

Cattaneo, E. R. "Time Sharing Seminar in Print," *Data Processing Magazine*, VII, 9 (September, 1965), 18-23.

Coleman, David and Theodore Cohn. "Some Specialized Uses of Data Processing Centers," *Management Services*, II, 5 (September, 1965), 40-46.

"Computers: A Delayed Revolution," *Business Week*, No. 1503 (June 21, 1958), 68-72, 76-78, 80, 85, 87, 90, 92.

"Computed Time Sharing Goes on the Market," *Business Week*, No. 1892 (December 4, 1965), 116.

Corcoran, G. J. "The Use of a Computer Service Bureau by Small Corporations," *National Office Management Association Management Bulletin*, III, 6 (December, 1962), 9-13.

Cross, J. A. "Protecting Client Records," in *Proceedings of the May 23-24, 1964, Management Symposium* (Abington, Pennsylvania: Association of Data Processing Service Organizations, 1964), 46-51.

"Data Processing Service Centers (Computer Centers)," *Dun's Review and Modern Industry*, LXXXVII, 1, Part 2 (January, 1966), 136-37.

Davies, Maurice B. T. "The Impact of Electronic Data Processing on Relationships Between Banks and CPAs," *The Journal of Accountancy*, CXX, 1 (July, 1965), 60-62.

Davis, Stanley. "A Client Looks at a Service Bureau," in *Proceedings of the January 21, 1963, Management Symposium* (Abington, Pennsylvania: Association of Data Processing Service Organizations, 1963), 12-16.

Dean, Neal J. "The Automated Services Division: A Key Profit Center," in *Proceedings of the 1964 National Automation Conference* (New York: The American Bankers Association, 1964), 79-85.

De Luca, A. Richard. "Understanding Total Systems," in *Total Systems* (Detroit: American Data Processing, Inc., 1962), 30-33.

Dudas, J. F. "On-Line Inquiry with Real-Time Answers," in *Data Processing*, VIII (Philadelphia: Data Processing Management Association, 1965), 48-51.

Dwyer, Edmund D. "Some Observations on Management Information Systems," in *Advances in EDP and Information Systems* (New York: American Management Association, 1961), 14-18.

"Electronics in the Office," *The Accountant*, CLIII, 4724 (July 3, 1965), 25-26.

Elliott, J. Richard, Jr. "Program For Growth?," *Barron's* XLIV, 12 (March 23, 1964), 3, 12, 14, 16, 18, 20, 23, 25.

——————. "Flourishing Think Factories," *Barron's* XLV, 38 (September 20, 1965), 3, 12-14, 16, 18.

Evans, W. H. "Data Processing For Others," in *Data Processing Yearbook* (Detroit: American Data Processing, Inc., 1963), 148-52.

"The Field of Management Accounting," *NAA Bulletin*, XLIV, 10, Section 3 (June, 1963), 3-22.

Fishbach, Joseph W. "Service Center Data Processing for the Business Community," *California Management Review*, IV, 1 (Fall, 1961), 35-50.

Genzlinger, Vance. "A Computer Philosophy For Smaller Businesses," *Data Processing Magazine*, VI, 12 (December, 1964), 17-20.

——————. "On Line Real Time *vs.* Time Sharing," *Data Processing Magazine*, VII, 3 (March, 1965), 40-41.

——————. "Package Systems and the Automobile Dealer," *Data Processing Magazine*, VII, 8 (August, 1965), 40-41.

Gilchrist, Bruce. "The Service Bureau Industry," *Datamation, V, 1* (January, 1964), 31-32.

Glaser, E. L., and F. J. Corbato. "Introduction to Time-Sharing," *Datamation,* X, 11 (November, 1964), 24-27.

Goodman, L. A. "Kolmogorov-Smirnov Tests for Psychological Research," *Psychological Bulletin,* LI (March, 1964), 160-68.

Greenberger, Martin. "Banking and the Information Utility," *Computers and Automation,* XIV, 4 (April, 1965), 28-31.

Harmon, R. L. "Versatility Spearheads Giant Service Center," *Computers and Data Processing Management,* I, 12 (December, 1964), 21-24.

Head, Robert V. "Banking Automation: A Critical Appraisal," *Datamation,* XI, 7 (July, 1965), 24-28.

Hendrich, James S. "Management Information Systems in Focus," in *Advances in EDP and Information Systems* (New York: American Management Association, Inc., 1961), 19-23.

Horngren, Charles T. "How Should We Interpret the Realization Concept?," *The Accounting Review,* XL, 2 (April, 1965), 323-33.

IBM's Answer to Time-Sharing," *Business Week,* No. 1854 (March 13, 1965), 50.

"Information Becomes a Hot Item," *Business Week,* No. 1915 (May 14, 1966), 64-166.

Isaacson, Bernard B. "Special Report to Council Alerts Practitioners to Computer Challenge," *The CPA,* XLV, 5 (June, 1965), 6-7.

Konstans, Constantine. "Partners in Profit," *The Michigan CPA* XVI, 5 March-April, 1965), 17-26.

Kovalinka, John W. and J. G. Trentin. "Management Information Systems," *Management Services,* II, 5. (September-October, 1965), 27-39.

Kranzley, Arthur S. "The Bank of the Future," *Datamation,* XI, 7 (July, 1965), 39, 42-43.

Lennox, John E. "How CPAs Can Adapt to the Computer," *The New York Certified Public Accountant,* XXXV, 12 (January, 1966), 893-98.

Lewis, J. W., "The Management of a Large Commercial Computer Bureau," *The Computer Journal,* VII (January, 1965), 255-61.

Long, Robert H. "Data Processing Service Opportunities in Banking," *ADAPSO Management Guidon,* V, 2 (March, 1965), 8-12.

Lynch, W. A., "When, Why and How to Undertake Program Development," *ADAPSO Management Guidon,* V, 4 (July, 1965), 7-11.

Magnis, N. E. "Time Sharing: A User's Perspective," *Data Processing Magazine,* VII, 7 (July, 1965), 26-29.

Mellema, J. Franklin. "The New Philosophy in Pricing Bank Services," *Auditgram,* LXII, 1 (January, 1966), 10-11, 36-38.

Mitchell, George W. "Effects of Automation on the Structure and Functioning of Banking," *The Journal of Accountancy*, CXXI, 3 (March, 1966), 60-61.

Moravec, Adolph F. "Basic Concepts For Designing a Fundamental Information System," Management Services, II, 4 (July-August, 1965), 37-45.

_____. "Basic Concepts For Planning Advanced Electronic Data Processing Systems," *Management Services*, II, 3 (May-June, 1965), 52-60.

_____. "Using Simulation to Design a Management Information System," *Management Services*, III, 3 (May-June, 1966), 50-58.

Moss, Morton F. "Management Services and the CPA Examination," *The Accounting Review*, XXXVII, 4 (October, 1962), 730-40.

Neuendorf, Charles W. "New Dimensions in Management Information," *Data Processing*, VI (Detroit: Data Processing Management Association, 1963), 42-49.

"A New Look at Data Processing Service Centers," *Modern Office Procedures*, VIII, 12 (December, 1963), 19-22.

Oh, George. "Automation, the Banks and the CPA," *The California CPA Quarterly*, XXXIII, 3 (December, 1965), 8-11, 38.

Palmer, Leonard J. "A Seller's Market for Data Processing Services," in *Proceedings of the January 21, 1963, Management Symposium* (Abington, Pennsylvania: Association of Data Processing Service Organizations,, 1963), 5-7.

Parisi, Salvatore. "Managing the Service Center," in *Proceedings of the February 19, 1962 Management Symposium* (Abington, Pennsylvania: Association of Data Processing Service Organizations, 1962), 7-12.

Patrick, A. W. and C. L. Quittmeyer. "The CPA and Management Services," *The Accounting Review*, XXXVIII, 1 (January, 1963), 109-17.

Patrick, Robert L. "Contracting For Computer Services," *Datamation*, VIII, 2 (February, 1962), 21-23.

Pfenning, R. E. "Business Information Systems," *The Accounting Review*, XXXVIII, 2 (April, 1962, 234-43.

Powell, James O. "What Makes a Service Center?," *Computer and Data Processing Management*, I, 12 (December, 1964), 25-26.

Reistad, Dale L. "Selecting and Selling Automated Services," *Banking*, LVII, 2 (August, 1964), 58, 60.

_____. "The Impact of Automation on the Nation's Banks," *Banking*, LVII, 4 (October, 1964), 51-56.

_____. "The Impact of Automation on the Nation's Banks," *Banking*, LVII, 5 (November, 1964), 106-109.

"Remote Accounting." *Computer News*, IX, 5 (May, 1965), 6-7.

Robinson, Herbert W. "Worth Waiting For: The Multiple Access Computer," *Data Processing Magazine*, VII, 9 (September, 1965), 40-42, 51.

Shays, E. Michael. "The Feasibility of Real Time Data Processing," *Management Services*, II, 4 (July-August, 1965), 19-29.

Slimak, Romuald. Comments in the *Proceedings of the January 20, 1961, Management Symposium* (Abington, Pennsylvania: Association of Data Processing Service Organizations, 1961), 5.

Smith, Arnold P. "Choosing a Service Bureau," *Computers and Automation*, XIII, 12 (December, 1964), 23-24.

Sprague, Richard E. "Information Utilities," *Financial Executive*, XXXIII, 10 (October, 1965), 56-61.

Tatham, Laura. "British Bureaux in Demand," *Data and Control* (October, 1964), 27-30.

"Tax Returns—By Computer," *The Journal of Accountancy*, CXIX, 2 (February, 1965), 23-24, 26-27.

"Time Sharing—Some Questions Answered," *Computer News*, IX, 12 (December, 1965), p. 2-3.

Trueblood, Robert M. "Accounting and New Management Attitudes," *The Journal of Accountancy*, CVI, 4 (October, 1958), 37-42.

——————————. "From Prediction to Preparation," *The CPA*, XLV, 9 (November, 1965), 2.

Waherspoon, G. M., Jr. "Message of Welcome," in *Proceedings of the January 20, 1961, Management Symposium* (Abington, Pennsylvania: Association of Data Processing Service Organizations, 1961), 3.

"What Management Consultants Can Do," *Business Week*, 1847 (January 23, 1965), 88-90, 92, 94, 96-98, 102, 104.

"What Can a Service Center Do For You?," *Computers and Data Processing,*, I, 3 (March, 1964), 40-43.

Wittus, Erwin Bud. "A CPA Firm's Experience With Punched Tape," *The Journal of Accountancy*, CXII, 3 (September, 1961), 65-70.

Unpublished Material

Shuster, H. John. "Marketing Data Processing Services to National CPA Firms." An unpublished paper presented to the May, 1965, ADAPSO Management Symposium.

Sparling, William Edward. "Data Processing Service Organizations: A Review of Their History and an Analysis of Their Use." Unpublished Ph.D. dissertation, State University of Iowa, 1961.

American Accounting Association's Committee to Prepare a Statement of Basic Accounting Theory. "A Statement of Basic Accounting Theory." East Lansing, Michigan, 1966 (Mimeographed.)

Other

"How to Choose and Use an Outside Service Bureau," Management Report, File 32 (New York: The Research Institute of America), September 4, 1962.

Raineri, Joseph. "Computer Service Industry," A Market Analysis Prepared for the firm of Steiner, Rouse and Company of New York City. January, 1966.

"Report KD-3 The Keydata System—A General Description." Cambridge: Keydata Corporation, 1965.

The Service Bureau Corporation, New York. Correspondence with James C. Reilly, Public Relations Director, dated March 15, 1966.

"Should You Use a Data Center?" *The Systemation Letter: No. 171.* Tulsa, Oklahoma: The Foundation for Administrative Research, 1965.

"Time Sharing System Scorecard," a pamphlet of Computer Research Corporation, Belmont, Massachusetts, Fall, 1965.

"What if . . .," A descriptive brochure of C-E-I-R, Washington, D. C.

Footnotes

CHAPTER I

1. "Computers: A Delayed Revolution," *Business Week* (June 21, 1958), p. 69.
2. John L. Carey, "The Impact of Computers on Practice," *The CPA* (March, 1965), p. 3.
3. Edwin T. Boyle, "What the Computer Means to the Accounting Profession," *The Journal of Accountancy* (January, 1966), p. 56.
4. Bernard B. Isaacson, "Special Report to Council Alerts Practitioners to Computer Challenge," *The CPA* (June, 1965), p. 7.
5. Robert M. Trueblood, "From Prediction to Preparation," *The CPA* (November, 1965), p. 2.
6. F. W. McRae, *The Impact of Computers on Accounting* (London: John Wiley and Sons, Ltd., 1965), p. vii.
7. Felix Kaufman, *Electronic Data Processing and Auditing* (New York: The Ronald Press Company, 1961), p. 3.

CHAPTER II

1. Harold Bierman, Jr., *Financial and Managerial Accounting: An Introduction* (New York: The Macmillan Company, 1963), p. 3.
2. C. Orville Elliott and Robert S. Wasley, *Business Information Processing Systems* (Homewood, Illinois: Richard D. Irwin, Inc., 1965), p. 16.
3. Bierman, *op. cit.*, p. 3.
4. Elliott and Wasley, *op. cit.*, p. 23.
5. Joseph Becker and Robert M. Hayes, *Information Storage and Retrieval: Tools, Elements, Theories* (New York: John Wiley and Sons, Inc., 1963), p. 3.
6. Elliott and Wasley, *op. cit.*, p. 16.
7. Ned Chapin, *An Introduction to Automatic Computers* (2d ed.; Princeton, New Jersey: D. Van Nostrand Company, Inc., 1963), p. 220.

8. Robert H. Gregory and Richard L. Van Horn, *Automatic Data Processing Systems: Principles and Procedures* (2d ed.; Belmont, California: Wadsworth Publishing Company, Inc., 1963), p. 3.
9. *Ibid.*, p. 516.
10. *Ibid.*, p. 576.
11. American Accounting Association, A Statement of Basic Accounting Theory (Evanston: American Accounting Association, 1966), p. 9.
12. Edmund D. Dwyer, "Some Observations on Management Information Systems," *Advances in EDP and Information Systems,* AMA Management Report Number 62 (New York: American Management Association, 1961), p. 17.
13. American Accounting Association, *op. cit.*, p. 12.
14. Richard F. Neuschel, *Management by System* (New York: McGraw-Hill Book Company, Inc., 1960), p. 212.
15. *Ibid.*
16. *Accounting Terminology Bulletin No. 1* (New York: American Institute of Certified Public Accountants, 1953), p. 9.
17. Robert M. Trueblood, "Accounting and New Management Attitudes," *The Journal of Accountancy* (October, 1958), p. 38.
18. *Ibid.*, p. 39.
19. See Edgar O. Edwards and Philip W. Bell, *The Theory and Measurement of Business Income* (Los Angeles: University of California Press, 1964).
20. Trueblood, *op. cit.*, p. 39.
21. "The Field of Management Accounting," *NAA Bulletin,* Section 3 (June, 1963), p. 4.
22. American Accounting Association, *op. cit.*, p. 41.
23. W. J. Bates, "Business Systems in Transition," *Data Processing for Management* (March, 1963), p. 20.
24. A. Richard DeLuca, "Understanding Total Systems," *Total Systems* (Detroit: American Data Processing, Inc., 1962), p. 31.
25. *Ibid.*
26. *Ibid.*
27. Vance Genzlinger, "A Computer Philosophy for Smaller Businesses," *Data Processing* (December, 1964), p. 19.
28. Adolph F. Moravec, "Basic Concepts for Planning Advanced Electronic Data Processing Systems," *Management Services* (May-June, 1965), p. 53.
29. *Ibid.*, p. 53.
30. Adolph F. Moravec, "Basic Concepts for Designing a Fundamental Information System," *Management Services* (July-August, 1965), p. 40.
31. Genzlinger, *op. cit.*, p. 19.

32. Wayne S. Boutell, "Business Oriented Computers: A Frame of Reference," *The Accounting Review* (April, 1964), p. 308.

33. J. F. Dudas, "On-Line Inquiry with Real-Time Answers," *Data Processing*, VIII (Philadelphia: Data Processing Management Association, 1965), 48.

34. E. Wainwright Martin, Jr., *Electronic Data Processing: An Introduction* (1st ed., Homewood, Illinois: Richard D. Irwin, Inc., 1965), p. 12.

35. Joseph Becker and Robert M. Hayes, *op. cit.*, p. 230.

36. Boutell, *Auditing With the Computer* (Los Angeles: University of California Press, 1965), p. 9.

37. James D. Gallagher, *Management Information System and the Computer* (New York: American Management Association, 1961), p. 17.

38. John W. Kovalinka and J. G. Trentin, "Management Information Systems," *Management Services* (September-October, 1965), p. 30.

39. James S. Hendrich, "Management Information Systems in Focus," *Advances in EDP and Information Systems* (New York: American Management Association, Inc., 1961), p. 19.

40. Boutell, *op. cit.*, Chapter 2.

41. *Ibid.*, p. 17.

42. Charles W. Neuendorf, "New Dimensions in Management Information," *Data Processing*, VI (Detroit: Data Processing Management Association, 1963), 48.

43. John L. Carey, *The CPA Plans for the Future* (New York: American Institute of Certified Public Accountants, 1965), p. 219.

44. Robert Beyer, "Management Services—Time for Decision," *The Journal of Accountancy* (March, 1965), p. 43.

45. John L. Carey, *The Concept of Management Services by CPAs* (New York: American Institute of Certified Public Accountants, 1959), p. 14.

46. Robert Beyer, *op. cit.*, p. 43.

47. John L. Carey, *The CPA Plans for the Future* (New York: American Institute of Certified Public Accountants, 1965), p. 235.

48. John L. Carey, *The Concept of Management Services by CPAs* (New York: American Institute of Certified Public Accountants, 1959), pp. 4 and 5.

49. Beyer, *op. cit.*, p. 47.

50. Beyer, *op. cit.*, p. 48.

CHAPTER III

1. "Automatic Data Processing—Services by Suppliers of Equipment," *Dun's Review and Modern Industry* (January, 1966), p. 131.

2. Bruce Gilchrist, "The Service Bureau Industry," *Datamation* (January, 1964), p. 31.

3. Leonard J. Palmer, "A Seller's Market for Data Processing Services," *Proceedings of the January 21, 1963, Management Symposium* (Abington, Pennsylvania: Association of Data Processing Service Organizations, 1963), p. 8.

4. *Ibid.*

5. "What Can a Service Center Do for You?," *Computers and Data Processing* (March, 1964), p. 41.

6. J. Richard Elliott, Jr., "Flourishing Think Factories," *Barron's* (September 20, 1965), p. 3.

7. "Data Processing Service Centers (Computer Centers)," *Dun's Review and Modern Industry* (January, 1966), p. 136.

8. William Edward Sparling, *Data Processing Service Organizations: A Review of Their History and an Analysis of Their Use* (Unpublished Doctoral dissertation, State University of Iowa, 1961), p. 44.

9. *Ibid.*

10. Enoch Haga (ed.), *Understanding Automation* (Elmhurst, Illinois: The Business Press, 1965), p. 83.

11. Ned Chapin, *An Introduction to Automatic Computers* (2d ed.; Princeton, New Jersey: D. Van Norstrand Company, Inc., 1963), p. 181.

12. Sparling, *op. cit.*, p. 47.

13. Sparling, *op. cit.*, p. 48.

14. *Ibid.*

15. Haga, *op. cit.*, p. 83.

16. Sparling, *op. cit.*, p. 48.

17. *Ibid.*, p. 50.

18. Haga, *op. cit.*, p. 96.

19. J. Richard Elliott, Jr., "Program for Growth?," *Barron's* (March 23, 1964), p. 3.

20. Elliott, "Flourishing Think Factories," *Barron's* (September 20, 1965), p. 3.

21. *Ibid.*

22. *Ibid.*

23. *Ibid.*

24. *Ibid.*

25. Elliott, "Program for Growth?," *Barron's* (March 23, 1964), p. 3.

26. Joseph Raineri, "Computer Service Industry," a Market Analysis Prepared for the firm of Steiner, Rouse and Company of New York City (January, 1966), p. 4.

27. G. M. Waherspoon, Jr., "Message of Welcome," *Proceedings of the January 20, 1961, Management Symposium* (Abington, Pennsylvania: Association of Data Processing Service Organizations, 1961), p. 3.

28. Romuald Slimak, comments in the *Proceedings of the January 20, 1961, Management Symposium* (Abington, Pennsylvania: Association of Data Processing Service Organizations, 1961), p. 5.

29. "By-Laws of the Association of Data Processing Service Organizations, Inc.," *Proceedings of the October 28 & 29, 1963, Management Symposium* (Abington, Pennsylvania: Association of Data Processing Service Organizations, 1963), p. 11.

30. *Ibid.*

31. Haga, *op. cit.*, p. 82.

32. Robert H. Long, "Data Processing Service Opportunities in Banking," *ADAPSO Management Guidon* (March, 1965), p. 8.

33. *Ibid.*, p. 9.

34. "Banks Open a New Window," *Business Week* (October 17, 1964), p. 158.

35. *Computer Research Study No. 1* (New York: American Institute of Certified Public Accountants, 1966), pp. 11 and 19.

36. See the complete results in Chapter V.

37. John E. Lennox, "How CPAs Can Adapt to the Computer," *The New York Certified Public Accountant* (January, 1966), p. 896.

38. R. L. Harmon, "Versatility Spearheads Giant Service Center," *Computers and Data Processing Management* (December, 1964), p. 21.

39. "Tax Returns-By Computer," *The Journal of Accountancy* (February, 1965), p. 23.

40. *Ibid.*

41. W. A. Lynch, "When, Why and How to Undertake Program Development," *ADAPSO Management Guidon* (July, 1965), p. 8.

42. *Ibid.*, p. 9.

43. Vance Genzlinger, "Package Systems and the Automobile Dealer," *Data Processing Magazine* (August, 1965), p. 40.

44. *Ibid.*

45. *Ibid.*, p. 41.

46. "What if . . . .," A descriptive brochure of C-E-I-R, Washington, D. C., pp. 14-17.

47. Donald F. Blumberg, "Role of the Service Bureau in Information Processing," *Proceedings of the October 15, 1962, Management Symposium* (Abington, Pennsylvania: Association of Data Processing Service Organizations, 1962), p. 7.

48. This section draws heavily from material in the Burroughs Corporation Manual, *Service Center Organization and Control.* I am much indebted to Mr. Leonard J. Palmer, its author.

49. Leonard J. Palmer, *Service Center Organization and Control* (Detroit: Burroughs Corporation, 1964), pp. 1-3.

50. James O. Powell, "What Makes a Service Center?," *Computer and Data Processing Management* (December, 1964), p. 26.

51. J. W. Lewis, "The Management of a Large Commercial Computer Bureau," *The Computer Journal* (January, 1965), p. 255.

52. Salvatore Parisi, "Managing the Service Center," *Proceedings of the February 19, 1962, Management Symposium* (Abington, Pennsylvania: Association of Data Processing Service Organizations, 1962), p. 7.

CHAPTER IV

1. H. John Shuster, "Marketing Data Processing Services to National CPA Firms," An unpublished paper presented to the May, 1965, ADAPSO Management Symposium.

2. Walter Camenish, Comments in the *Proceedings of the January 20, 1961, ADAPSO Management Symposium* (Abington, Pennsylvania: Association of Data Processing Service Organizations, 1961), p. 18.

3. Shuster, *op. cit.*

4. Constantine Konstans, "Partners in Profit," *The Michigan CPA* (March-April, 1965), pp. 25-26.

5. "Remote Accounting," *Computer News* (May, 1965), p. 6.

6. David Coleman and Theodore Cohn, "Some Specialized Uses of Data Processing Centers," *Management Services* (September-October, 1965), pp. 48-49.

7. Erwin Bud Wittus, "A CPA Firm's Experience With Punched Tape," *The Journal of Accountancy* (September, 1961), p. 65.

8. *Ibid.*, p. 67.

9. See Vance Genzlinger, "Package Systems and the Automobile Dealer," *Data Processing Magazine* (August, 1965), pp. 40-41.

10. Laura Tatham, "British Bureaux in Demand," *Data and Control* (October, 1964), p. 30.

11. Charles S. Abbott, "Buy, Lease, Share a Computer—Or Utilize a Service Bureau?" *Computers and Automation* (February, 1960), p. 15.

12. *Ibid.*

13. Reprint of "A New Look at Data Processing Service Centers," *Modern Office Procedures* (December, 1963), p. 2.

14. This section was suggested by Arnold P. Smith, "Choosing a Service Bureau," *Computers and Automation* (December, 1964), pp. 23-24.

15. G. J. Corcoran, "The Use of a Computer Service Bureau by Small Corporations," *National Office Management Association Management Bulletin* (December, 1962), p. 12.

16. "Should You Use a Data Center?" *The Systemation Letter: No. 171*, 1965, p. 2.

17. Smith, *op. cit.*, p. 24.

18. Robert L. Patrick, "Contracting for Computer Services," *Datamation* (February, 1962), p. 21.

19. *Ibid.*, p. 22.

20. *Ibid.*

21. Letter from James C. Reilly, The Service Bureau Corporation, New York, March 15, 1966.

22. Coleman and Cohn, *loc. cit.*

23. *Management of an Accounting Practice: MAP 18* (New York: American Institute of Certified Public Accountants, 1963), pp. 15-16.

24. This section draws heavily upon *Electronic Data Processing: V—The Use of Computer Service Bureaux* (London: The Association of Certified and Corporate Accountants, 1964), pp. 14-17.

25. *Ibid.*, p. 14.

26. *Ibid.*, p. 15.

27. J. A. Cross, "Protecting Client Records," *Proceedings of the May 23-24 Management Symposium* (Abington, Pennsylvania: Association of Data Processing Service Organizations, 1964), p. 48.

28. Joseph W. Fischbach, "Service Center Data Processing for the Business Community," *California Management Review* (Fall, 1961), p. 40.

29. Shuster, *op. cit.*, p. 14.

30. *Ibid.*

31. "How to Choose and Use an Outside Service Bureau," Management Report File 32, *op. cit.*, p. 8.

32. Konstans, *op. cit.*, p. 23.

33. Leonard J. Palmer, "A Seller's Market for Data Processing Services," *Proceedings of the January 21, 1963, Management Symposium* (Abington, Pennsylvania: Association of Data Processing Service Organizations, 1963), p. 8.

34. *Computer Research Study No. 3: Computer Applications to Accounting Operations* (New York: The American Institute of Certified Public Accountants, 1966), pp. 13-14.

35. Stanley Davis, "A Client Looks at a Service Bureau," *Proceedings of the January 21, 1963, Management Symposium* (Abington, Pennsylvania: Association of Data Processing Service Organizations, 1963), pp. 12-16.

36. *Ibid.* p. 13.

37. *Computer Research Study No. 3: Computer Applications to Accounting Operations* (New York: The American Institute of Certified Public Accountants, 1966), pp. 14-15.

CHAPTER V

1. Interview with William Ludwig, formerly Executive Director of the Michigan Association of Certified Public Accountants, February 16, 1966.

2. Based upon the estimates of computer manufacturers' local representatives, the vast majority of computerized Michigan banks fall well within the resource limit established by the fiftieth largest bank.

3. A second mailing was necessary to increase the response from 60 percent of the population to the 80 percent attained.

4. Pecuniary considerations dictated that follow-up letters be sent to certain categories of involved firms only. Their initial response was low relative to their proportion of the population. This action partially accounts for the comparatively skewed response distribution of the second phase of the survey as opposed to the response distribution of the first phase.

5. The following question was asked: "Please indicate the size of the largest city within 20 miles of your office or the size of the city in which your office is located, whichever is larger."

6. See Appendix D for explanation of statistical measures used.

7. For clients served, $D = .462$; for gross annual billings, $D = .476$; for staff size, $D = .636$; hence, all imply that the distribution for the non-involved firms is stochastically larger. See Appendix D.

8. See Appendix B for the definition of management services employed in the study.

9. See Appendix B for the definition of systems and procedures employed in the study.

10. $D = .438$, which implies that the distribution for the non-involved firms is stochastically larger. See Appendix D.

11. $D = .487$, which implies that the distribution for the non-involved firms is stochastically larger. See Appendix D.

12. A Chi-square test was employed using the data contained in Table V-15. Chi-square $= 10.31$, with the probability of getting such a value less than .01.

13. A survey conducted by the Lansing sales office of IBM found 17 computerized banks in Michigan offering service bureau-type services.

CHAPTER VI

1. Robert V. Head, "Banking Automation: A Critical Appraisal," *Datamation* (July, 1965), pp. 25-26.

2. Neal J. Dean, "The Automated Services Division: A Key Profit Center," *Proceedings of the 1964 National Automation Conference* (New York: The American Bankers Association, 1964), p. 83.

3. Dale L. Reistad, "The Impact of Automation on the Nation's Banks", *Banking* (October, 1964), p. 51.

4. Dale L. Reistad, "The Impact of Automation on the Nation's Banks", *Banking* (November, 1964), p. 107.

5. Dale L. Reistad, "Selecting and Selling Automated Services," *Banking* (August, 1964), p. 58.

6. Maurice B. T. Davies, "The Impact of Electronic Data Processing on Relationships Between Banks and CPAs," *The Journal of Accountancy* (July, 1965), p. 61.

7. Reistad, "Selecting and Selling Automated Services," *Banking* (August, 1964), p. 58.

8. Dean, *op. cit.*, p. 82.

9. J. Franklin Mellema, "The New Philosophy in Pricing Bank Services," *Auditgram* (January, 1966), p. 11.

10. George W. Mitchell, "Effects of Automation on the Structure and Functioning of Banking," *The Journal of Accountancy* (March, 1966), pp. 60-61.

11. John W. Allen, *et al., Marketing Your Bank Computer Services Profitably* (Boston: Warren Gorham and Lamont, Inc., 1965), p. 6.

12. M. B. Basson, "Expanded Bank Services Through Automation: Opportunity or Trap?," *Proceedings of the 1964 National Automation Conference* (New York: The American Bankers Association, 1964), p. 248.

13. Davies, *op. cit.*, p. 60.

14. Arthur S. Kranzley, "The Bank of the Future," *Datamation* (July, 1965), p. 42.

15. *Ibid.*

16. Reistad, "The Impact of Automation on the Nation's Banks," *Banking* (October, 1964), p. 54.

17. *Ibid.*

18. *Directory of Bank Automation* (Park Ridge, Illinois: NABAC, The Association for Bank Audit, Control and Operation, 1966), p. 4.

19. Davies, *op. cit.*, p. 61.

20. *Ibid.*

21. George Oh, "Automation, the Banks and the CPA," *The California CPA Quarterly* (December, 1965), p. 9.

22. John E. Lennox, "How CPAs Can Adapt to the Computer," *The New York Certified Public Accountant* (December, 1965), p. 895.

23. For an excellent summary of recommended action for the profession and individual CPAs, see Maurice B. T. Davies, *op. cit.*, p. 62.

25. Herbert W. Robinson, "Worth Waiting For: The Multiple Access Computer," *Data Processing Magazine* (September, 1965), pp. 40-42, 51.

25. Charles W. Adams, "Man-Machine Collaboration," in *Data Processing Yearbook* (Detroit: American Data Processing, Inc., 1965), p. 76.

26. *Ibid.*
27. E. R. Cattaneo, "Time Sharing Seminar in Print," *Data Processing Magazine* (September, 1965), p. 19.
28. *Ibid.*
29. Walter F. Bauer, "On-Line Systems—Their Characteristics and Motivations," Reprint from *On-Line Computing Systems* (Detroit: American Data Processing, Inc., 1965), p. 6.
30. Robert V. Head, *Real-Time Business Systems* (Holt, Rinehart, Winston, Inc., 1964), p. 3.
31. *Ibid.*
32. *Ibid.*, p. 5.
33. E. Michael Shays, "The Feasibility of Real Time Data Processing," *Management Services* (July-August, 1965), p. 21.
34. Head, *op. cit.*, pp. 264-74.
35. "Time Sharing System Scorecard," a pamphlet of Computer Research Corporation, Belmont, Massachusetts (Fall, 1965), p. 4.
36. "Computer Time Sharing Goes on the Market," *Business Week* (December 4, 1965), p. 116.
37. *Ibid.*
38. Donald F. Blumberg, "Time Sharing: Some Comments and Predictions," *Data Processing Magazine* (September, 1965), p. 44.
39. E. L. Glaser and F. J. Corbato, "Introduction to Time-Sharing," *Datamation* (November, 1964), p. 25.
40. *Ibid.*, p. 26.
41. *Ibid.*
42. *Report KD-3, The Keydata System—A General Description* (Cambridge: Keydata Corporation, 1965), pp. 7-11.
44. *Ibid.*, pp. 6, 10, and 11.
45. *Ibid.*, p. 11.
46. *Ibid.*
46. This section was suggested by Vance Genzlinger of the Detroit CPA firm of Plante and Moran.
47. Charles W. Adams, "Man-Machine Collaboration," *Data Processing Yearbook, 1965* (Detroit: American Data Processing, Inc., 1964), p. 78.
48. Vance Genzlinger, "On Line Real Time *vs.* Time Sharing," *Data Processing Magazine* (March, 1965, p. 41.
49. N. E. Magnis, "Time Sharing: A User's Perspective," *Data Processing Magazine* (July, 1965), p. 28.
50. "Information Becomes a Hot Item," *Business Week* (May 14, 1966), p. 164.
51. "Time Sharing—Some Questions Answered," *Computer News* (December, 1965), p. 3.

52. Richard E. Sprague, "Information Utilities," *Financial Executive* (October, 1965), p. 56.

53. *Ibid.*

54. *Ibid.*

55. "IBM's Answer to Time-Sharing," *Business Week* (March 13, 1965), p. 50.

56. Martin Greenberger, "Banking and the Information Utility," *Computers and Automation* (April, 1965), p. 31.

57. Charles T. Horngren, "How Should We Interpret the Realization Concept?," *The Accounting Review* (April, 1965), p. 324.

58. *Ibid.*

59. Adolph F. Moravec, "Using Simulation to Design a Management Information System," *Management Services* (May-June, 1966), pp. 50-58.

PUBLICATIONS OF THE DIVISION OF RESEARCH

AGRICULTURAL MARKET ANALYSIS
Vernon L. Sorenson, editor

LABOR MARKET INSTITUTIONS AND WAGES IN THE
LODGING INDUSTRY
John P. Henderson

THE EXECUTIVE IN CRISIS
Eugene Emerson Jennings

BANKING STRUCTURE IN MICHIGAN: 1945-1963
Robert F. Lanzillotti

RETAIL DECENTRALIZATION
Eli P. Cox and Leo G. Erickson

BANK ADMINISTERED POOLED EQUITY FUNDS FOR
EMPLOYEE BENEFIT PLANS
Frank L. Voorheis

THE PERFORMANCE POST AUDIT IN STATE GOVERNMENT
Lennis M. Knighton

PASSENGER TRANSPORTATION
Stanley C. Hollander

THE EFFECTS OF DATA-PROCESSING SERVICE BUREAUS ON
THE PRACTICE OF PUBLIC ACCOUNTING
Constantine Konstans

INSTITUTE FOR INTERNATIONAL BUSINESS AND ECONOMIC
DEVELOPMENT STUDIES

MSU International Business and Economic Studies

MICHIGAN'S COMMERCE AND COMMERCIAL POLICY STUDY
John L. Hazard

INTERNATIONAL DIMENSIONS IN BUSINESS
Recent Readings from BUSINESS TOPICS

MANAGEMENT DEVELOPMENT AND EDUCATION IN THE SOVIET UNION
Barry M. Richman

THE UNITED STATES OVERSEAS EXECUTIVE: HIS
ORIENTATIONS AND CAREER PATTERNS
Richard F. Gonzalez and Anant R. Negandhi

STEEL AND ECONOMIC DEVELOPMENT: CAPITAL-OUTPUT
RATIOS IN THREE LATIN AMERICAN STEEL PLANTS
David G. Greene

ALTERNATIVE COMMERCIAL POLICIES — THEIR EFFECT
ON THE AMERICAN ECONOMY
Mordechai E. Kreinin

INSTITUTION BUILDING IN BUSINESS ADMINISTRATION—
THE BRAZILIAN EXPERIENCE
Donald A. Taylor

THE OPTIMAL STAGING AND PHASING OF MULTI-PRODUCT CAPACITY
Harold H. Wein and V. P. Sreedharan

INSTITUTE OF PUBLIC UTILITIES

MSU Public Utilities Studies

DEVELOPMENT OF SEPARATIONS PRINCIPLES IN THE
TELEPHONE INDUSTRY
Richard Gabel

PERFORMANCE UNDER REGULATION
Harry M. Trebing, editor

MID-CONTINENT AREA POWER PLANNERS
W. Stewart Nelson